Sugen Gopal

ROTI KING

Classic and Modern Malaysian Street Food

Sugen Gopal

ROTI KING

Classic and Modern Malaysian Street Food

Photography by Sam Folan

Quadrille

CONTENTS

INTRODUCTION

The first Roti King restaurant opened in Euston, London, in 2014 but the story of Roti King started much earlier. It isn't possible to pinpoint exactly when, as I didn't really break into the food world, it was just where I grew up.

My parents ran restaurants, and the smells and sounds from those kitchens were the foundation of my childhood. I'm from Ipoh in Malaysia – a city with a thriving food scene and, in my opinion, some of the most delicious food in the world. Malaysian cuisine is so varied and interesting, influenced by the techniques and flavours of the diverse population of immigrants who come to the country from across the globe.

My parents opened a roadside café in Buntong, Ipoh, in the 1970s. It was a small spot under a tree with just a few tables. Positioned by a busy road near a school, the café became so popular they eventually had to close it because the traffic it attracted became unmanageable. The little spot under the tree was later demolished (the only trace of it is the floor tiles pictured on page 10), but they had created a following of people keen to eat their food. They hadn't set out to expand, but their popularity demanded it. So, they took on a double unit just across the road from their original spot. Ipoh was a flourishing city at the time, and executives would bring their clients to our restaurant, alongside other groups, often made up of businessmen who would come to eat after playing golf. It had air conditioning (always welcome in Malaysia!) and another big sitting hall upstairs. There were very few restaurants like this at the time in Ipoh, so it became very popular – Gopal's Corner was born. My parents were both very hard working, believing that if you owned a restaurant you needed to always be there running the show and never missing service. No holidays, no leisurely weekends – the restaurant was the epicentre of our lives.

My mum was a powerhouse in the kitchen. Among the 20 or so dishes they served each day, one of their most well-known ones was the Fish-head Curry (see page 66). Looking back, this was quite a thrifty idea – my dad would pick up fish heads from the market for free, and my mum would make them into curry. It became the dish that people would keep coming back for. I'd often be in the kitchen as an extra pair of hands for my mum, to help lift heavy pots, stir curries and assist her with general prep. The way she cooked influenced me hugely, and it is how I cook now – most ingredients were added by eye and she wasn't overly prescriptive with timings. She'd shout instructions to add a pinch of this or a handful or that and I'd have to keep asking her for the next direction, or for her to check if a dish was ready or needed to cook for longer. I was an extra pair of hands – I wasn't at that point being trusted to really cook. It meant I didn't grow up with a set of recipes handed down to me, so for years after setting up on my own, I'd often have to call her to ask questions. Watching her run the kitchen showed me how much energy and love goes into making good food.

While mum was always the great cook (something she inherited from my maternal grandfather), dad was front of house and had a keen interest in food. He'd take me to all the best spots in our region, in search of new dishes, sometimes driving for hours just to try a specific meal. I've inherited his love of seeking out delicious food. The restaurant became even more of a family affair when my dad's siblings started helping there. I began working there when I was ten years old, making the drinks. We were encouraged to work before and after school and at weekends, and we could use our earnings to pay for school kit and anything else we needed.

The restaurant was always busy, with everyone rushed off their feet. So, when I turned 14 my dad needed me to be more useful and suggested I learn to make roti canai. At that time, my uncle, Kanna Mama, was the master of roti-making and I really had to convince him to teach me – he wasn't willing to take the time to train me up unless I was properly engaged. As payback for his tutelage, I had to make him coffee first thing in the morning and wash his car! I spent months and months mixing dough, 25kg (55lb) at a time, before I was allowed to reach the next step – to throw a roti (and it's my uncle's method that I include on page 28). Roti canai are made from simple ingredients but the process to prepare the dough involves practise; the technique of stretching and slapping to make the dough paper-thin is a skill to master.

After many months of training, I was trusted to make roti on quiet mornings before I left for school. One day, when my uncle wasn't available, I stepped in to make the roti for the restaurant – and it went well. From then on, at 5 o'clock every morning before school, then after school in the evenings and every weekend, I made the roti in the restaurant. The customers loved it and thought it was great to see someone so young able to hone the craft. And I haven't stopped making roti since! As a teenager I'd never have believed that making roti would become my success story. Having seen how hard my parents worked, I hadn't planned on following in their footsteps and running a restaurant, but sometimes life has other plans...

In 2004 I opened a small kiosk in Oriental City, a food hall in Colindale, north London. Both my brother (who'd soon joined me in the UK) and I started making and selling roti. After a trip back to Malaysia to get married, I returned to London and found that the spot at Oriental City had been given to someone else. At this point I very nearly gave up – I couldn't find work and I was running out of money. A friend offered me a job in a jeans factory in Leeds, so I booked a bus ticket to leave London. But after a chance meeting with the kiosk owner, I found out that the spot was available again and he asked if I'd like it back. I didn't have enough money to pay the rent but I had an instinct to give it one last shot.

That evening, before I was due to leave for Leeds to start again, I had a talk with my brother. Would he help me if I took over running a food kiosk at Oriental City? He was adamant we should go to Leeds; he reminded me that we had always said we wouldn't have a restaurant of our own, like our parents. But something was telling me that this was a good opportunity and I somehow convinced him to stay in London and figure this out. I knew I could make it work, we just had to give it a go and I'm so glad we took that risk together.

There was just the matter of rent payment to work out. The owner helped me negotiate paying rent monthly rather than settling the conventional 12 months upfront. I decided I had one year to make a go of it at Oriental City. I remember this so well as it really was the turning point – I had just £80 in my pocket and the chance to set up my own roti stall. I went out and bought as much rice, meat and vegetables as I could with the money I had. The next day, on 5 November 2004 (a date I'll always remember!), we opened, serving only rice and curry. Customers at Oriental City were wondering where the roti was but I didn't have the funds to buy the hot plate or griddle I needed, so the 'roti stall' I'd started wasn't even serving roti! A fellow trader, who had eaten my roti before, ended up lending me the cash (without me asking him or agreeing how and when I'd pay him back) and I've never forgotten this kind gesture.

I stayed at Oriental City for four years and when it closed, I set up several more stalls in other London locations. It was difficult to sustain market stalls for very long, sometimes even being forced to close because I was too busy and unwittingly stealing business from other traders. Years later, in 2012, it was when I was selling roti at East Ham Market that a customer called me the Roti King – a throwaway compliment that stuck. He was from Jamaica (where roti are a staple) and he didn't believe I could make them as delicious as he was used to. As soon as he ate my roti, though, he declared it the real deal and he was so excited he shouted, 'You are the Roti King!'. It's him that I have to thank for my name, as I liked the title so much, I decided to keep it.

Many iterations later, I was offered a space in London's Chinatown, where I started selling reasonably priced lunches. It became popular, and just as I was growing a good lunchtime following, I arrived to work one day to yet another setback – the shop was shut. It turned out the landlord was a gambler and he hadn't paid the rent. The property manager kindly told me that I could have the key and continue to trade for the day so that I had some capital to start afresh somewhere new. I opened the shop and sold everything, but I decided to pay all of the staff the outstanding salaries the owner had failed to. The property manager said I should have used the money to start somewhere new but that didn't sit well with me. So, once again, I was left without any money or a premises to trade from, but I wasn't to be defeated.

Shortly after, in 2014, I was offered a new space – a failing Chinese restaurant with cheap rent at 'Chinese Euston' on 40 Doric Way, a bustling part of central London. This became the original Roti King and taking this on was the start of the success that we know now. I didn't have the capital for a bells-and-whistles refurbishment and I wasn't confident enough to drop the existing menu, not wishing to risk losing any of our longstanding customers. So, I kept the restaurant décor as it was and continued serving some of the Chinese dishes already on the menu. Before long, it became busy and the lunchtime crowd were coming for my roti. I kept my prices low as I wanted to appeal to the masses, including the customers who'd followed me from Chinatown. Ten years on, my approach remains the same and I believe it's better to have a short menu of trusted dishes at reasonable prices that people keep returning for.

It was once I was settled in Euston that the popularity of our food really rocketed. Marina O'Loughlin, then restaurant critic at *The Guardian*, gave us an amazing review and word spread that there was this little, unassuming spot that was serving the best roti in town. I remember the first couple who came in after that review. I didn't recognize them as regulars and when we got chatting, they showed me the review in the paper. They cheeringly warned me that the crowds would follow a review like that and I was

excited at the prospect of a few extra customers off the back of it, but what happened was much bigger. A queue formed the next day, and for the next few weeks I wondered if it would stop – ten years later, it hasn't.

Looking back now, it was a crazy time – stressful and exciting in equal measure. The sight of people lining up for my food, then eating and enjoying it, was such a buzz (and still is!). Reaching a new level of popularity overnight meant we had to keep up with demand. My team and I worked long days to serve the never-ending customers. I was working round the clock, keeping across all elements of the business as well as training new staff. We'd often run out of cutlery and glasses, and sometimes we'd even run out of food. I would have to ask the front of house to shut the door at 8pm as I couldn't physically serve any more. My brother came back from Malaysia to help, and since then we've stayed working together – we've expanded around the city to three other sites, and even launched an iteration of our parents' original restaurant, Gopal's Corner, that is a celebration of Malaysian Tamil food. And, after all this time, the Roti King in Euston continues to be our most popular spot.

Whenever I do events now and I see queues, I love it. That's all I want. The sight of a queue gives me a buzz, a natural high. It's my favourite part of my job, seeing people queue for my food, to eat it and to enjoy it.

After all these years, the core menu is still the same – you can come and have a quick lunch of roti and kari at a very decent price. We still use high-quality, fresh ingredients sourced locally and I believe that is part of the secret to our success. We now make over 5,000 roti per day at Roti King and each and every one is made with love.

My journey to where Roti King is today is a story of trial and error, but ultimately perseverance. And the same goes for making roti – if you're keen to make your own you will also need to persevere, but as long as you cook with love, the outcome will be delicious.

MALAYSIAN COOKING

Malaysian cuisine is vibrant and flavoursome and has been greatly influenced – in terms of ingredients used, flavour combinations and cooking techniques – by neighbouring countries: Thailand and Indonesia, and beyond. Malaysia is made up of a diverse demographic, with just over half of the population being Malay, around a quarter Chinese and many Indian. Immigration, historic trading routes and colonization have all influenced the variety of ingredients and methods of cooking that make Malaysian cuisine what it is. We'll be looking at some of these influences in many of the recipes in this book, from roti canai, originally brought to Malaysia from South India, to noodles and Hainanese chicken from China.

Cooking from scratch is an important aspect of Malaysia's food culture. I describe Malaysian food as genuine because, to me, using fresh ingredients is fundamental. Families generally take great pride in cooking and recipes are passed down through generations, tweaked and adapted along the way to get better and better. Every meal is there to nourish, and food is used as a means to bring people together, with celebrations always centered around feasting.

STREET-FOOD CULTURE

How we eat in Malaysia is just as important as what we eat, and it's the street-food culture that has proved a huge inspiration to me in setting up Roti King. Street food is an intrinsic part of life for many in Malaysia – whether you want a hot meal, a savoury or sweet snack or a reviving drink, whatever time of day, there are a huge variety of options available.

Generally, the food available from the roadside in Malaysia is really good – it's fast food but cooked fresh. Roadside street vendors and hawker market stalls sell a mix of fried, steamed and boiled meat and fish, flavoured with an abundance of vegetables, herbs, spices and aromatics. There are rice and noodle dishes that are cooked quickly in front of you using fresh ingredients, as well as curries that have

been made from scratch. Malaysian cuisine makes use of the diverse fresh ingredients and spices that are so readily available across the country.

All sorts of people rely on street food, from manual workers grabbing breakfast from 6am onwards to office staff nipping out for a snack during the day, and families visiting night markets looking for a tasty dinner. It's delicious, affordable and you'll always find something to satisfy your cravings. Lots of the all-day snacks are packaged and wrapped in clever ways, making them easy to grab and go. One of them – the anchovy sambal (known as Sambal Ikan Bilis, see page 133) – is a classic Malaysian all-day breakfast offering that you'll find wrapped in a banana leaf in a cone shape.

What we eat at different mealtimes in Malaysia is a bit of a free-for-all. While in the West meals tend to look quite different at breakfast, lunch and dinner, in Malaysia the distinction is less rigid. Roti and kari, for example, are just as popular at breakfast as they are later in the day. Mobile hawker stalls are able to move around and offer their fare to anyone, anywhere, at any time. No one minds where they're eating at a given time of day, they're just happy to be fed. It's a very different way of thinking about dining and eating out on the go than what we are used to in the West.

Coffee shops (*kopitiams*) are also a popular option and are found pretty much everywhere. They're usually surrounded by street-food stalls, often with the coffee-shop owners renting spaces to stall vendors. It's mutually beneficial – customers buy a coffee at the kopitiam and order some food from a stall, with the kopitiams providing tables and chairs to use. Night markets are another amazing food experience, always buzzing with activity, a riot of colour and noise. Whenever I'm on a visit home, I always take a trip to Ipoh night market on a Friday evening – even if I'm not hungry! It's a place full of good vibes and always the best spot to catch up with friends. To me, this market feels the same as it's always been and I love the fact that I recognize vendors who have been cooking the same dish for 20 or 30 years as a family. It's a real experience, and one I love to return to.

MY STREET-FOOD MEMORIES

Growing up, as well as eating in my parents' restaurant, I ate most of my meals at roadside stalls. Often there wouldn't be a menu, instead the vendors would cook their speciality dish and I'd know to expect something full of flavour. That's how our family ate together and also how we made a living, so it is a huge part of my childhood and the driving force behind Roti King.

The beauty of the street food I grew up eating rests on two things. Firstly, the vendors made small quantities of food, using fresh ingredients, which made it taste all the better. Secondly, because there were (and continue to be) so many options, and therefore so much competition, the sellers have to keep their food first rate if they're to rely on repeat custom. Great street food needs to taste like home.

The number of street-food options lining the streets in Malaysia is a testament to the population's entrepreneurial spirit. Street-food stalls provide an essential role in society but they also serve a key economic function, as a way for many to make a living. Becoming a street-food vendor is easy, it requires minimal start-up costs and low continued outgoings, and offers everyone a chance to make some money for their family. In fact, the sellers are always a family business – the elders, with years of experience, will be doing the cooking and the kids will be out touting for custom.

As long as you have the confidence to cook, all you need is an idea and a table to serve from. The spirit of street-food vendors is one I've kept with me through the Roti King journey.

USING THIS BOOK

This book is a collection of my interpretations of my favourite dishes, as well as the dishes that keep people coming back to Roti King in London time and time again. Some of these recipes are my take on classic Malay dishes and Malay street food, others I have created myself using ingredients more readily available in the UK. Even within Malaysia, the food served will change depending on the area you're in, as with any cuisine. I love the way that food travels and the idea of others buying this book to create Roti King dishes and Malaysian-style food for themselves.

I also encourage you to make the recipes your own. Don't worry about authenticity – we have to cook to please our own tastes and those we're cooking for. It's worth noting that the roti that I was taught to make were square-shaped, but I decided to serve round rotis in my restaurants! That is my way and no one would suggest they're inauthentic. Although my mum taught me how to cook, I also believe that a lot of what I've learned, and the way I cook now, is thanks to my curiosity to try new things. I believe the best cooking is made up of both skill and inspiration. If you try something that someone else has cooked and you love it, try to make it yourself and then make it your own.

If you are new to Malaysian cooking, and in particular to making roti, please remember that these are skills you may not grasp straight away. As I've mentioned, I learned the craft over many years when I started throwing roti as a small boy. You can't expect to perfect it the first time, but I promise you the more you practise, the better your roti will be. Don't give up.

Sugen Gopal
London, 2025

INGREDIENTS & KITCHEN EQUIPMENT

There's a common misconception that Malaysian cooking is complicated, and perhaps this is due to the abundance of spices and homemade pastes we use. Happily, I'm here to tell you that's not the case. In this section I'll be showcasing the ingredients and equipment used in Malaysian cookery, to assure you that it's easier than you may think!

Let's talk ingredients. There are a handful of ingredients that are integral to the flavours of Malaysia that you will use again and again, such as tamarind, shrimp paste, lemongrass and, of course, chilli, garlic, ginger and onion. You may find you already have some of the other frequently used aromatics in your cupboards, such as cinnamon, cardamom, star anise and clove. This combination is used in so many dishes and it's worth including all of them, if you can – see The Malaysian Pantry, on the following pages, for a more detailed list.

As a general note, I prefer to use pure ingredients as much as possible. Working as a chef, the main reason for this is flavour: fresh, unprocessed ingredients taste better. We're all becoming more aware of the damage that fast- and ultra-processed foods have on our health, and that cooking from scratch is much better for us. Yes, we can buy long-lasting garlic, ginger and tamarind paste from supermarkets, but they contain other additives to make them keep for so long. Similarly, while sambals and other curry pastes can be picked up from supermarket shelves, when we make our own, we know exactly what ingredients are in them.

When it comes to how you cook these recipes at home, you won't need lots of specialist kit. The majority of Malaysian street-food dishes are straightforward to make, as they're designed to be prepared on the roadside. There are a mix of recipes in this book, from quick meals you can make in less than 20 or 30 minutes after work to some longer, more involved dishes that you might save for the weekend. I also include suggestions throughout for what you might cook on celebratory occasions and other events, like a barbecue for family or friends – see page 169 for Banana Leaf Meals, for a celebration feast.

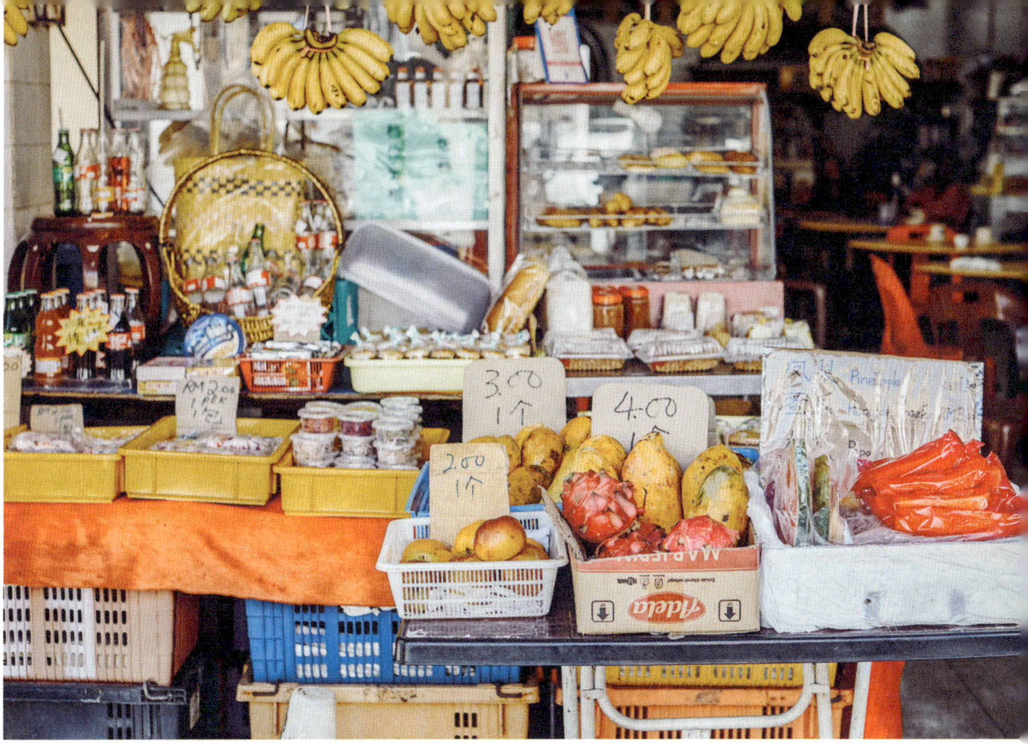

RM 2.00
1 PEK
3.00
1个
4.00
2.00
1个
Adela

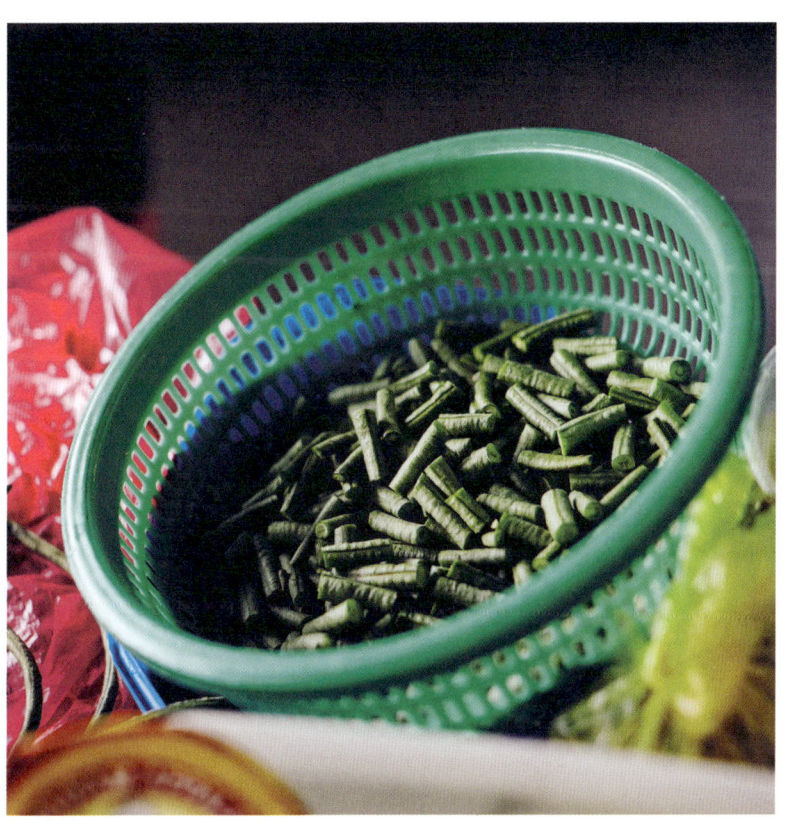

THE MALAYSIAN PANTRY

The staples I use throughout this book are mostly available from regular supermarkets, although there are a few slightly more specialist items that you can source from Asian supermarkets or online. I list some of my favourite brands in this section but if you're unable to get hold of specific products, just use what you can find (many recipes suggest ingredient swaps that you can make). You might be surprised to see ingredients like tomato ketchup used in recipes such as Ayam Masak Merah (see page 86) and malt vinegar in Hainanese Chicken Rice (see page 90), but these just go to show the Western influence on Malaysian food.

BEANSPROUTS

The best beansprouts in the world are from my hometown Ipoh. The unique texture and flavour are a result of the fresh spring water in their cultivation. In the UK, the best-quality beansprouts can be found in Asian supermarkets, but if you're buying them from the supermarket try to find the freshest you can.

CHILLIES

The biggest change I've made to my cooking since leaving Malaysia is in the balance of heat, generally dialling down the quantity of chilli I use in order to cater to different tastes. It's a massive challenge when cooking with chillies to get the heat levels right, as the heat from both fresh and dried chillies varies enormously. There are hundreds of chilli varieties available, and I recommend you try as many as possible to find the ones you prefer. My advice is to buy chillies from your local greengrocer or supermarket, taste them, and start to learn their heat levels.

Throughout the book when I refer to a fresh red chilli, I mean the standard chilli you'd find in a supermarket, often sold in mixed packets of green and red. Some recipes call for smaller, hotter bird's eye chillies, which vary in heat – to get a sense of their heat level, have a taste and if it's super spicy use it very sparingly. Green 'finger' chillies are often hotter than regular green chillies and provide a good level of heat. When a recipe calls for dried chillies, I use dried Kashmiri as standard but other types of dried chillies are ok to use too, if that's what you have. I recommend Kashmiri because the heat is consistent and other dried chillies might be too spicy. The sambal recipes include both fresh and dried chillies, which adds a unique flavour – it's worth sourcing both if you can. You can remove the seeds from both fresh and dried chillies if you want to bring down the heat levels. If you aren't sure about the spice level, it's always better to add less, taste and add more if you like. Too much or too little chilli can ruin a meal. I also use Kashmiri chilli powder as standard; I would recommend trying to source this, too, if you can.

COCONUT

Many of my recipes specify fresh or frozen shredded coconut – Shana is a good brand of frozen coconut. If using frozen coconut, defrost it by soaking it in water before draining, then scrunch it in your hands to remove any excess moisture. If you are using canned coconut milk, try to avoid the 'light' options and check the coconut content in the ingredients to ensure it is high – I'd recommend Aroy-D. I also like to use coconut cream as a block; it keeps well and is more economical than fresh. The block can be added to sauces instead of canned, and used to replace fresh coconut in dishes such as Rendang, on page 56.

CONDENSED MILK

This is used in several of the sweet recipes in the book as well as the Roti Canai (see page 35), where you'll have leftovers, which you can decant and keep refrigerated or freeze. If keeping in the fridge, check the can for storage instructions, but most brands are fine left in an airtight container in the fridge for up to a month (if not longer). If you freeze condensed milk, give it a good mix once defrosted as some separation may occur.

CRISPY FRIED SHALLOTS

A lot of Malaysian dishes are topped with crispy fried shallots, which have a crunchy texture and a sweet flavour. I give instructions on page 142 as to how to make your own, but if you'd rather use store-bought that's fine (just don't skip them altogether!). It's important to keep the cooking oil if you are making your own, as this can be used to add flavour once you've finished cooking – I will instruct you where to add the oil as well as the shallots. Please use my instructions on the amount of crispy fried shallots to top your dishes with as a guide – you can always add more if you like.

CURRY LEAVES

Try to buy fresh curry leaves, which are becoming increasingly available in supermarkets, rather than dried (that have much less flavour). Remove the stalks and freeze the leaves – these will be fine frozen for six months.

DRIED ANCHOVIES

Ikan bilis, as they're called in Malaysia, are fished from the sea, and immediately boiled in salt water by the fishermen and left to dry naturally. I particularly love them as a snack fried with peanuts (see page 123) and they're also the key ingredient for Sambal Ikan Bilis (see page 133). Look out for Jeeny's – often sold in south-east Asian supermarkets.

DRIED SHRIMPS

These small shrimps have been cooked, salted and dried in the sun. They can be found in larger bags in Asian supermarkets and they keep, well sealed, in the fridge. I'd recommend BDMP or Jeeny's.

GALANGAL

This root is from the same family as ginger and it is used in many south-east Asian recipes to give a spicy, citrussy flavour. In the UK, galangal can be harder to source fresh, so instead you can use a paste (just check the contents and try to find one with the least amount of extra ingredients added).

HERBS

Fresh coriander is often added to dishes towards the end of the cooking time, or as a garnish. Chives are also common, usually added to soups and broths.

LEMONGRASS

In my opinion, this is an underestimated ingredient. Lemongrass (as the name suggests) is a type of grass that grows all over Malaysia and is a common ingredient for cooking and infusing in teas. It's a plant that we believe has many healing properties and benefits to the body. I love using lemongrass in my recipes, both for its flavour and aroma. It's often added to seafood dishes to help mask the fishy smell – a trick I learned from my mum. It's usually best to remove the outer layer of the lemongrass stick, as well as its thinner top end. The bottom root part of lemongrass sticks are more tender and they need to be bashed before use to release their flavour and aroma. This is the part of the lemongrass stick we add to lots of the pastes that make up the recipes in this book. You can save the thinner tops and add them to the Rendang recipes on page 54.

LIME LEAVES

As with curry leaves, lime leaves should be bought fresh or frozen if possible. If you are using the lime leaves in a paste, the stalks should always be removed because they are often very tough. When they are added to a sauce whole, the stalks can be left on.

OIL, GHEE AND BUTTER

Most of my recipes use a light neutral oil, usually vegetable unless otherwise stated. Occasionally ghee or butter is used too. Butter is unsalted, unless otherwise stated.

ONIONS, SHALLOTS, GINGER AND GARLIC

These key ingredients make up the foundations of so many dishes in this book. In most recipes, onions and shallots can be used interchangeably, allowing you to use whichever you have to hand. I suggest you make a jar of both Ginger Paste (see page 138) and Garlic Paste (see page 138) and keep them in the fridge – far superior to store-bought pastes, which often contain additives. As a general rule, 1 large garlic clove makes 1 teaspoon of garlic paste. If you don't have a batch of paste ready to go when making a recipe, just mince the ginger or garlic as needed.

PANDAN LEAVES

Pandan is a grass that's found everywhere in Malaysia. Its leaves give a subtle aromatic flavour to all sorts of dishes, from rice, where it's tied in a knot and added during cooking, to sweet dishes – you'll find it in the No-churn Coconut and Pandan Ice Cream (see page 148). It's best to buy fresh leaves and freeze them – avoid pandan essence. If you're unable to get hold of pandan leaves, just omit from the recipe altogether.

RICE AND NOODLES

Before we talk about all the exciting flavours of Malaysian cuisine and produce, a note on rice. Rice is a mainstay of most Malaysian meals, and it's rare that a bowl of steamed white rice won't be served as an accompaniment. The rice I cook is always white, and long grain; however, some recipes call for basmati and I would always serve white basmati alongside a Banana Leaf Meal (see page 169). I also like to serve jasmine rice with the Hainanese chicken on page 90. Our most internationally known dish, nasi lemak, is centred around a generous helping of aromatic coconut rice, with lots of extras to accompany it, such as spicy sambal, cooling cucumber, crunchy peanuts and egg for a hit of protein. Most Malaysians eat with their hands (a common practice in many parts of south-east Asia), whereby rice becomes a crucial vehicle for absorbing sauces.

For the noodle dishes in this book, I recommend using a couple of different types of noodles. Mamak Mee Goreng (page 50) uses egg noodles, which are sold ready to use and are available in most supermarkets. Char Kway Teow (see page 47) and Ipoh Kuey Teow Soup (see page 76) use flat rice noodles, which are sold both cooked or uncooked (either is fine, just adapt the cooking time accordingly). They can be found in Asian supermarkets and are gluten-free.

SAMBALS AND PASTES

The backbone of Malaysian cooking includes sambals and spice pastes, which provide punches of flavour to every dish. Common across south-east Asia, they tend to be made in large quantities as they are used so often and keep well in the fridge. The Basic Sambal recipe (see page 132) features in many of the recipes throughout this book, and although you can buy a jar from a shop, I recommend you make your own. When using pastes, it's important to cook them until you see the oil separate from the paste – you'll know when it has been cooked for long enough when the colour turns a deeper red.

SHRIMP PASTE

Fermented shrimp paste is often used in south-east Asian cooking, adding a salty fishy flavour. It works particularly well with the morning glory in the Kangkung Belacan (see page 43), which is a bestseller at Roti King. Shrimp paste, often labelled 'belacan', comes in two different forms, either in a dried block or in a small pot of ready-to-use paste. The dried block should be toasted in a frying pan before using; my favourite brand is Jeeny's. Many prefer the pre-toasted shrimp paste, because toasting your own is an extremely smelly activity and the aroma will linger in your kitchen for days. Malaysians have many tricks to mask the smell, but if you are new to cooking with belacan I suggest buying the ready-to-use paste if you can; my favourite brand is Jeeny's.

SPICES

Whole spices are used regularly in this book, such as cardamom pods, cloves, cinnamon sticks and star anise, which act as aromatics for curries and rice dishes. In Malaysia, we'd usually serve dishes with these whole spices still intact, but you can remove them if you prefer. I recommend freshly grinding your own spices as and when you need them using a pestle and mortar or an electric spice grinder, as whole spices tend to stay fresher for longer, but you can use ready-ground if you prefer. A rough rule of thumb is that 1 teaspoon of whole spices, such as coriander, cumin and fennel, is equal to 1½ teaspoons of ground. I like to buy large packets of spices from Asian supermarkets from brands that I know, but wherever you buy your spices, the important thing is to always make sure they're fresh. Old spices lose their aromatic properties, becoming useless.

SPICE MIXES

Often spices are ground and combined – these spice mixes are frequently used throughout the recipes. Here are a few of the most common blends used:

- The Roti King Spice Mix (see page 134) is used in several recipes throughout the book, and I really recommend you make a batch and keep it in a jar ready to add to dishes.

- Sambar is an integral spice mix in many dishes, and I like the brands Aachi and Babas.

- Garam masala is a blend of toasted spices such as cinnamon, cloves, ginger, cardamom and black pepper. You can make your own or buy it ready-mixed from most supermarkets.

TAMARIND

This is an essential ingredient in Malaysian cooking and it is included in many of the recipes in this book. The sweet-sour paste is extracted from the pods of the tamarind fruit and its acidity cuts through rich flavours. I recommend trying to get hold of a block of wet, seedless tamarind, then mix it with water to make a paste. You then strain it to remove the husks with your hands, leaving you with a tamarind juice that is ready to cook with. I use different ratios of tamarind block to water before straining, depending on how strong I want the finished juice to be. Ready-to-use tamarind concentrate can vary greatly, so if you are buying it rather than making it, look for the highest concentration of tamarind to water and try to avoid any products with citric acid or vinegar added. As tamarind pastes vary so widely, I suggest you add a little at a time and taste as you go.

TOFU

Fried bean curd (tofu) puffs used in the Mamak Mee Goreng and Taugeh Ikan Masin on pages 50 and 65 are commonly used in Malaysian cooking and can be found in Asian supermarkets, alongside dried tofu sticks, which are used in the Spicy Coconut Mackerel on page 81.

STORE-CUPBOARD ESSENTIALS

While the staples listed on the earlier pages can be switched out for other ingredients if needed, below are the essential ingredients that you should keep in stock ready to make the recipes in this book.

- **Chicken powder** – A much-used ingredient in my kitchen, my favourite brand is Honor, which is found in recognizable bright-yellow tubs. If you can't get hold of chicken powder, you could substitute it with chicken stock.

- **Chinese cooking wine/Shaoxing wine** – This is made from fermented rice and used in lots of Chinese-influenced dishes.

- **Curry powder and fish curry powder** – These are both used in my recipes. Try to source Malaysian curry powder if you can. If you can't get hold of fish curry powder, standard curry powder will be fine.

- **Dark caramel sauce** – A thick sauce found in Asian supermarkets and online, which is often labelled 'karamel masakan'. I like the Cheong Chan brand, which I use in a handful of recipes in this book, including Mamak Mee Goreng (see page 50) and the Hainanese Chicken Rice (see page 90).

- **Fish sauce** – This is made from fermented fish. Brands really vary and supermarket-own brands aren't always the best quality, so if you have access to an Asian supermarket, I suggest trying to get the Squid brand.

- **Light and dark soy sauce** – Both are made from fermented soya beans mixed with water and salt, but the light version is lighter in colour and saltier in taste than dark soy sauce, which is sweeter and richer. I specify in the recipes which to use, but light soy is generally my go-to. Tamari is a gluten-free alternative if you need to swap out either.

- **Oyster sauce** – A thick, salty sauce made from oyster extract, used predominantly in Chinese cuisine and across most south-east Asian countries. My favourite brand is Kum Kee.

- **Sugar** – I use both white caster (superfine) sugar and soft dark brown sugar in my cooking. We also use jaggery for the Sweet Roti on page 156, but you can substitute this with dark brown sugar if you don't have jaggery.

- **Tom yum paste** – I use this in the Ikan Bakar recipe (see page 84); I recommend the Mae Ploy brand.

FRESH MEAT, FISH & SEAFOOD

Try to source the best-quality meat you can afford (ideally free-range and/or organic). Always buy meat on the bone, if possible, which gives a better flavour.

- **Chicken** – Generally, I like to buy a whole chicken, then carve it up and freeze any parts I'm not using for later use. This should work out to be more economical and you can also make stock from the discarded parts and bones – see page 90 for instructions. If you prefer, you can buy the equivalent weight of your choice, just make sure to buy skin-on, bone-in cuts as this adds so much flavour.

- **Mutton and lamb** – Mutton is much better for curries, as it's a firmer meat with more fat. It's better suited to longer cooking than lamb and has a stronger flavour.

- **Fish** – As with chicken, use the whole fish rather than buying cuts – the flavour will be better and it's also more economical. Many of my white fish recipes are flexible regarding the type of fish used – see relevant recipes for specific notes.

- **Prawns (shrimp)** – You can use fresh prawns but frozen are usually slightly cheaper and are fine for most recipes. Try to buy shell-on if you can, and save the heads and shells for fish stock or the Fish-head Curry (see page 66). Prawn heads are full of flavour.

KITCHEN EQUIPMENT

The recipes in this book do not require much in the way of special equipment. That said, there are a few essential items that I would recommend:

- **Knives** – A sharp knife is the most important tool for any cook. Having a sharp knife not only speeds up the preparation process but it also makes it more enjoyable. There are many instructions to 'finely slice' ingredients in the upcoming recipes, made possible by a sharp knife. I instruct you to prepare meat, fish and shellfish yourself. A good pair of kitchen scissors alongside sharp knives is vital.

- **Pans** – Saucepans of varying sizes, along with frying pans, sauté pans and woks, are essential. Many of the stir-fried dishes in the book need a high heat for the dish to taste as it should, so good-quality pans that can withstand high temperatures are important.

- **Jars** – The Sambals & Extras chapter (see page 130) is full of recipes for pastes and sambals that can be made ahead and cooked later. It also includes recipes for condiments to complement other dishes in the book, which can be made in large quantities to use as and when you need them. I recommend storing them in sterilized jars, which are labelled and dated, and kept in the fridge to help them last well. To sterilize jars, preheat the oven to 150°C/130°C fan/300°F/gas 2. Wash the glass jars thoroughly in hot soapy water, removing the lids and any rubber sealants and washing them well too. Place the jars and lids on a clean baking sheet and warm in the oven for 5 minutes. Cool before filling them with your delicious pastes, sambals and condiments.

- **Blender** – A very good blender is needed to make pastes, which are used in so many of these recipes. Size doesn't matter so much here as you can always blitz in batches, but a powerful motor and a sharp blade are essential for blending pastes to a smooth enough consistency. A handheld stick blender is also a very useful bit of kit to have – always blend in a high-sided bowl or jug to avoid mess.

- **Rice cooker** – At home, I prefer to cook rice in a rice cooker – and as rice is served with most Malaysian meals, I get a great deal of use out of it. If you don't have one, just use a good-sized pan with a lid.

- **Pressure cooker** – Really useful to speed up when cooking pulses (among other things), I recommend using a pressure cooker for the dal recipes (see pages 45 and 98). If you don't have one, don't worry, I include instructions for cooking dal on the stove.

- **Freezer** – I am a massive fan of the freezer. Make the most of freezer space and pack it full of any ingredients you can't use up, rather than letting them languish in your fridge. Ingredients such as lemongrass, ginger and chillies all freeze incredibly well, either peeled and chopped or frozen whole.

GENERAL COOKING NOTES

Here I've included a few simple tips on how to get the best results while cooking from this book.

- **Taste, taste, taste** – As mentioned with regards to chilli, tasting your food as you cook is very important. The quality of meat, fish and vegetables varies enormously and so does the flavour. I have tried to give other cues of what to look out for, as well as timings with instructions for most cooking steps, but it's worth remembering that ingredients won't always behave in the same way. The more you taste your food, the better your understanding of your ingredients will be.

- **Prepare** – It's always best to read through the whole recipe before starting to cook so that there are no surprises once it's too late! I also recommend that you prep all the ingredients (as per the ingredients list instructions) before you start to cook. As lots of these street-food dishes cook very quickly over a high heat, it's really important to have your ingredients ready to throw in the pan at the right moment. It makes for a much more enjoyable cooking experience, too.

- **Order is key** – The order in which ingredients are added is very important. Please follow the instructions given; for example, onions will need to be cooked for longer than garlic – if both are added to the pan at the same time, the onion will end up undercooked and the garlic will burn. Adding ingredients in the correct order will result in the best flavour.

- **Cooking out pastes** – Many of the recipes call for a paste to be made, blended until smooth and then fried in a pan. It is difficult to give exact timings for this process, so it is important that you know when the paste has been fried for long enough and is sufficiently cooked. Often containing garlic, ginger and lemongrass, it's key these ingredients are thoroughly cooked out. The pastes are cooked in oil on a medium heat in a frying pan and it is important to stir them as they cook to avoid sticking or burning. The paste is ready when the oil starts to separate from the paste, and as soon as you see the oil separating you know the paste is ready and to carry on with the next step of the recipe. This step cannot be rushed.

KEY

Vegetarian and vegan recipes are highlighted throughout, just look out for the following symbols:

Vegetarian (V)

Vegan (VG)

ROTI KING CLASSICS

These are the dishes I've been cooking at Roti King since we opened ten years ago, the reliable favourites from our menu, and the rest I've been cooking since I was just ten years old at my parents' roadside restaurant. You'll learn how to make various rotis from scratch, as well as curries and dals and my hope is that you'll come back to these recipes again and again, as I have done.

ROTI CANAI

This chapter starts with my signature recipe for making perfect roti canai at home. 'Roti' translates to 'bread' and roti canai (pronounced cha-nigh) are fluffy, crispy and soft flatbreads. Similar to an Indian paratha (but unique in many ways), they're served alongside meat, fish or dal kari as the star of the Roti King show, and they make a wonderful accompaniment to most of the dishes in this book. As I described in the introduction, I was taught to make roti canai aged 14, practising before and after school and at weekends. My uncle taught me everything I know, and this recipe has been the foundation of my cooking career ever since. Roti are the ultimate Malaysian street-food offering and have always been my customers' favourite – I can't imagine a time that I won't be making and selling them!

Roti dough is classed as 'enriched', a term that refers to any dough whereby ingredients other than the standard flour, water and yeast are added (condensed milk, butter and sugar all go into roti dough). The dough is mixed, rested, divided and then stretched – the stretching of the dough is where the skill lies. I'll be walking you through the key stretching steps that get the roti super-thin, as this is what results in a soft and flaky roti. Before attempting this with the real dough, you can practise with a damp dish towel, just like I did all those years ago. The stretched dough is then folded before it's cooked, and these folded layers make the flatbread soft on the inside and crispy on the outside. It's a great thing to watch the speed at which a skilled roti maker throws and slaps the dough.

The recipe and method that follow makes plain roti, and once you've mastered the technique for this, the filled and sweet roti, which build from the same recipe method, will be easy. Please don't be put off by the lengthy instructions – the step-by-step directions will arm you with the skills needed to make perfect, delicious roti. As with most bread-making, practising again and again is the way to master the craft. The first attempt may not be perfect, but practise will help to improve the dough and, before you know it, you'll be making roti canai fit for a roti king or queen!

This recipe makes enough for ten roti. That may seem like a lot and you may not be planning to eat ten roti (though I wouldn't blame you if you did!), but they do keep – see below. You can, of course, halve the recipe to make five portions, but I'd suggest you make the full amount. If it's your first time making them, some of your roti may not make the cut as perfectly paper-thin (though to avoid food waste, the less-than-perfect roti dough can still be cooked and enjoyed!). At Roti King we serve two roti with most dishes.

Once you've completed the overnight rest stage, your roti will keep in the fridge in an airtight container or covered in cling film (plastic wrap) for up to three days. You could also freeze the dough at this stage – wrap each individual ball in cling film and store in the freezer for up to three months. To defrost, just leave at room temperature until soft and pick up at the 'stretch' stage outlined. Though the roti dough can be prepared in advance, roti must be served fresh when cooked.

Over the following pages, you'll see a breakdown of the steps for making roti canai, followed by more detailed instructions within the recipe.

A STEP-BY-STEP GUIDE

1. **PREPARE THE DOUGH**. Combine the ingredients, adding the butter or margarine a little at a time until the dough comes together.

2. **WORK THE DOUGH**. In a mixer, or with your hands, work the dough until you have a smooth ball.

3. **REST THE DOUGH AND THEN DIVIDE**. After its first rest of 30 minutes, divide the dough into 10 smooth balls. At Roti King, we use a technique that involves squeezing a large piece of dough out through the top of your fist, then pinching it off to create a ball. For the second rest, the dough balls are fine to sit next to each other touching.

4. **REST**. Thoroughly coat the balls with oil and leave to rest for 8 hours or overnight in the fridge.

5. **STRETCH**. As pictured below, on an oiled surface and with very oily hands, use your palm to stretch the dough outwards, to make a very large, thin sheet. The aim is to keep the dough at an even thickness – you shouldn't need to use much pressure from your hand as you glide the dough outwards.

6. **SLAP**. The tricky bit! As pictured below, the stretched dough should be extremely thin at this point, almost completely translucent. Aim for at least six slaps and don't worry if the dough folds over – just unfold it again. Similarly, you can fix any tears by bunching up the dough and smoothing over.

NOTE

If you are struggling with the slap technique, see **page 36** for a shortcut.

7. **FOLD**. Once you have a super-thin, translucent sheet of dough on your counter, fold in each side to the centre to make a square, creating air pockets as you fold – as below.

8. **COOK.** Just before frying, give it a final stretch out with your hands to bring it back to size (if left for a few minutes, it will have shrunk once folded). Add to the pan and wait for the all-important 'cracking' sound before flipping.

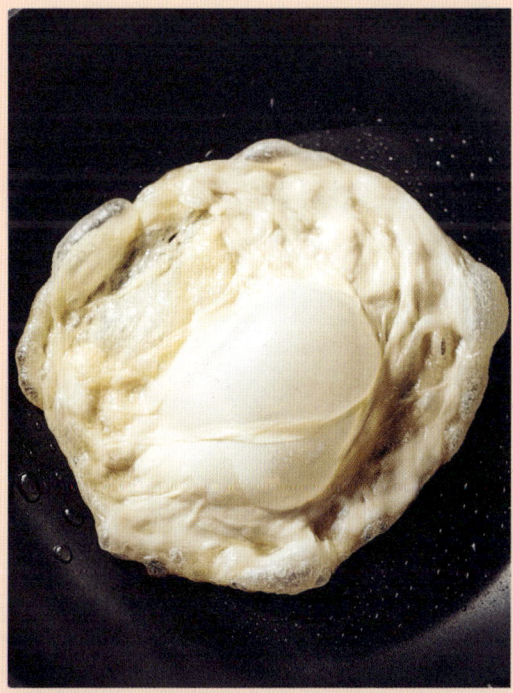

9. **CLAP**. Place the roti between your hands and 'clap' to transform it into a fluffy, crispy, flaky roti.

ROTI CANAI v

MAKES 10 ROTI
PREP TIME 10 MINUTES +
4.5 HOURS RESTING TIME
AND 30 MINUTES SHAPING,
DEPENDING ON YOUR
EXPERIENCE
COOK TIME 2–3 MINUTES
PER ROTI

2 tsp salt

2 tsp caster (superfine) sugar

1 tbsp condensed milk

500g (1lb 2oz) plain (all-purpose)
   flour

1 tbsp softened butter or
   margarine, plus extra butter
   for coating

vegetable oil, for coating

1. Using a stand mixer with a dough-hook attachment or a large bowl, combine the salt, sugar, condensed milk and 350ml (12fl oz) of warm water. Stir for 1 minute until the sugar and salt have dissolved. Add the flour and use your hands to mix everything together until the liquid and the flour have combined. Add the butter or margarine gradually in teaspoonfuls and keep mixing until a shaggy dough forms.

2. In a mixer (for 2–3 minutes) or by hand (for 4–5 minutes) keep bringing the mix together until the dough is smooth. If you've been using a stand mixer, now start working by hand. With well-oiled hands, work the dough in a circular motion, smoothing it out. The dough should be completely smooth and rounded with a shiny surface.

3. Cover with a coating of oil or butter and leave to rest for 30 minutes at room temperature. Divide the dough into 10 equal-sized pieces, each weighing approximately 70–75g (2½–3oz) – you can roll the dough into a sausage shape and then cut it into portions, weighing each one on scales as you go to ensure they're equal. Roll each piece into a smooth ball.

4. Use your hands to coat each ball in vegetable oil, then place them on a baking sheet, cover with cling film (plastic wrap) and leave to rest for at least 4 hours, or overnight, in the fridge. At this point, you could also wrap the dough balls individually in cling film and freeze for later use.

5. After the dough has rested, cover your work surface with a generous amount of oil – you really want to grease up the surface and your hands. This will help to stop the dough sticking to the surface or your hands. The following instructions need to be completed per ball of roti – you can either prepare and cook each roti one at a time or prepare all/half the balls ready to cook, leaving the remaining roti balls covered in the refrigerator – see pages 30–34 for step-by-step photographs of the method. Take the first ball and start to use the palm of your hand to push the dough in an outward motion. It's really important that you only use the palm of your hand and do not apply much pressure, or you'll create holes. The oil will help your hand to glide over the dough smoothly. The dough needs to be of a consistent thickness and remain in a roughly circular shape (it doesn't need to be a perfect circle as you're about to throw it). Keep adding oil so that there is no friction between your hands and the dough. You are aiming to carefully stretch the dough to about 35–40cm (14–16in), becoming thinner without creating any holes.

continued . . .

6. This step is the one to practise using a wet dish cloth. When you're ready to start with the real thing, consider the first few rotis to be further practise! Hold the edge of the dough nearest to you between the thumb and index finger of one hand, with the rest of your fingers resting on top of the dough. In a smooth, confident motion, pick up the edge of the dough with your other hand (a little further away from the hand already holding it), then quickly lift up the dough with both hands and slap it down on the work surface. Repeat this at least six times, moving your hands a little each time to rotate the dough after each slap, widening and stretching it in all directions. If you're struggling with the slap, try carefully stretching the dough by peeling the sides off the surface, lifting gently and stretching out the dough towards you a little at a time or see the shortcut below. Don't worry too much if the dough tears around the edges a little.

7. When the dough is as thin as you can get it, fold in the sides to make a square shape, roughly 25cm (10in). Fold each side quickly, trapping as much air as you can in the fold to create air pockets and bubbles. Then leave the folded roti to rest for 2–3 minutes while you heat the pan. You can either take all the roti you want to cook to this point and leave the prepared roti to rest on the surface, or cook one at a time.

8. Heat a large frying pan over a high heat and add ¼ teaspoon of oil. As the pan heats up, place the roti on the counter and stretch the dough back to a 15–20cm (6–8in) circle. Once the pan is hot, add the dough and you should hear a 'cracking' sound – this is important; if you don't hear it, the pan isn't hot enough. Once you hear a 'cracking', wait at least 30 seconds before flipping the roti over, flipping it four times in total. Each roti will take 2–3 minutes to cook if the pan is hot enough. It should be covered in brown spots as it cooks and you should see the roti puffing up.

9. Remove from the pan and put the cooked roti back onto your oiled countertop. Clap your hands together on either side of the roti and rotate it a few times as you do so. Do this 3–4 times and the roti will go from flat to flaky. Perfect!

SHORTCUT

If you are struggling with step 6 and the slap is not working for you, as well as using your hands to stretch out the dough on the surface, you can also use a rolling pin. Make sure the rolling pin is well oiled and after you have smoothed out the dough with your hands in step 5, simply use the rolling pin to stretch out the dough as thinly as you can.

ROTI MURTABAK

FILLED ROTI

These rotis are a signature Malaysian dish that owe their name to the artful folding process used to craft them. All kinds of fillings can be wrapped within the pillowy roti dough before pan-frying to crispy perfection. I've included three of my favourite fillings here, which are all delicious served sliced up with Roti King Dal (see page 45). The chicken or lamb masala makes enough to serve four on its own, if you don't use it as a filling.

These recipes follow the ingredients and method for Roti Canai on page 35, with the fillings added after the 'slap' and before the 'fold' stages (see pages 31–32 for a reminder). Generally, the fillings are added to the full surface area of the stretched-out roti and then the sides are folded in like an envelope into a square before being added to a hot frying pan to cook.

Each filling recipe makes enough for one serving (and one stretched-out roti), but they are all easily scaled up to feed more.

CHICKEN OR LAMB MASALA

MAKES 1 x FILLED ROTI

1 egg, whisked

1 tbsp finely diced red onion

1 x Roti (see page 35)

For the masala chicken or lamb (this filling makes enough to serve four on its own)

1 tbsp vegetable oil

1 onion, finely diced

2 tsp Garlic Paste (see page 138)

2 tsp Ginger Paste (see page 138)

500g (1lb 2oz) minced (ground) chicken or lamb

100g (3½oz) Onion Masala Paste (see page 139)

2 tsp salt

½ tsp ground turmeric

10 curry leaves, picked from the stalks

1 tsp garam masala

For the chicken or lamb masala, heat the oil in a large frying pan over a medium–high heat, add the onion and cook for 6–7 minutes until soft. Add the garlic and ginger pastes and cook for a further 5 minutes, stirring often.

Turn the heat up and add the mince to the pan, breaking it up with a wooden spoon. Stir continuously for 10–15 minutes until the mince is cooked and drying out. (If you are using lamb you will probably find that the meat is more moist and you may need to drain off some of the liquid from the pan in order for the meat to dry out.)

Add the onion masala paste, salt, turmeric, curry leaves and garam masala, and continue to fry for a further 5 minutes.

Cool the mixture before using it to fill the roti murtabak. You only need 1 tablespoon per roti, so you will have plenty leftover – it will keep in the fridge in an airtight container for three days.

Combine the egg, onion and 1 tablespoon of chicken or lamb mince masala over the outstretched dough once you reach step 7 on page 36.

Once folded, heat a large frying pan over a high heat and add ¼ teaspoon of oil. As the pan heats up, place the roti on the counter and stretch the dough back to a 15–20cm (6–8in) circle. Once the pan is hot, add the dough and you should hear a 'cracking' sound – this is important; if you don't hear it, the pan isn't hot enough. Once you hear a 'cracking', wait at least 30 seconds before flipping the roti over, flipping it four times in total. Each roti will take 2–3 minutes to cook if the pan is hot enough. It should be covered in brown spots as it cooks and you should see the roti puffing up.

Remove from the pan and put the cooked roti back onto your oiled countertop. Clap your hands together on either side of the roti and rotate it a few times as you do so. Do this 3–4 times and the roti will go from flat to flaky. Perfect!

SPINACH AND CHEESE v

MAKES 1 x FILLED ROTI

50g (1¾oz) cheddar cheese, grated

25g (1oz) baby spinach leaves

1 x Roti (see page 35)

¼ tsp vegetable oil

Sprinkle the grated cheese and spinach leaves over the outstretched dough once you reach step 7 on page 36.

Once folded, heat a large frying pan over a high heat and add ¼ teaspoon of oil. As the pan heats up, place the roti on the counter and stretch the dough back to a 15–20cm (6–8in) circle. Once the pan is hot, add the dough and you should hear a 'cracking' sound – this is important; if you don't hear it, the pan isn't hot enough. Once you hear a 'cracking', wait at least 30 seconds before flipping the roti over, flipping it four times in total. Each roti will take 2–3 minutes to cook if the pan is hot enough. It should be covered in brown spots as it cooks and you should see the roti puffing up.

Remove from the pan and serve hot.

EGG AND ONION v

MAKES 1 x FILLED ROTI

1 egg, whisked

1 tsp finely diced red onion

1 x Roti (see page 35)

salt and pepper, to taste

¼ tsp vegetable oil

Mix together the egg, onion and seasoning in a small bowl and pour this over the outstretched dough once you reach step 7 on page 36.

Once folded, heat a large frying pan over a high heat and add ¼ teaspoon of oil. As the pan heats up, place the roti on the counter and stretch the dough back to a 15–20cm (6–8in) circle. Once the pan is hot, add the dough and you should hear a 'cracking' sound – this is important; if you don't hear it, the pan isn't hot enough. Once you hear a 'cracking', wait at least 30 seconds before flipping the roti over, flipping it four times in total. Each roti will take 2–3 minutes to cook if the pan is hot enough. It should be covered in brown spots as it cooks and you should see the roti puffing up.

Remove from the pan and serve hot.

GULAI TUMIS

TAMARIND FISH KARI

This is a popular dish in Malaysia, where most households have their own version. This was originally taught to me by my mum and I've tweaked it over the years. If you want to prep ahead, you can make the sauce the day before, keeping it in the fridge once cool then following the final step of the method when you are ready to cook the fish – in fact, this dish actually tastes better the next day. The tamarind makes the fish hot, spicy and sour, and the sauce is perfect for roti-dipping and/or served with rice, which will absorb it.

SERVES 4–6
PREP TIME 10 MINUTES
COOK TIME 1 HOUR
10 MINUTES

3 tbsp vegetable oil

3 shallots, finely sliced

7 tsp salt

2 tbsp Garlic Paste (see page 138)

6 tbsp fish curry powder (see page 22)

½ tsp fenugreek seeds, toasted

2 fresh green chillies, stalks removed and halved lengthways

8 curry leaves

3 medium tomatoes, roughly chopped

½ tsp ground turmeric

1 tsp Kashmiri chilli powder

50g (1¾oz) tamarind block mixed with 150ml (5fl oz) warm water

1 tsp caster (superfine) sugar

110ml (3½fl oz) coconut milk

1 king fish (use the whole fish – approx. 800g/1lb 12oz or 600g/ 1lb 3oz if using fillets), chopped into large 4–5cm (1½–2in) chunks (see note)

200g (7oz) okra, topped and tailed

1 tsp Roti King Spice Mix (see page 134)

1 fresh green chilli, halved lengthways

Add 2 tablespoons of oil to a large pan and set over a medium heat. Add the shallots and 1 teaspoon of the salt and cook for around 10 minutes, until the shallots are soft and starting to turn golden. Remove from the pan and blitz in a blender until smooth. Add the blended shallots back to the pan with the garlic paste and cook out for 5 minutes over a medium heat. Prepare the curry powder by mixing it in a small bowl with 150ml (5fl oz) of boiling water to make a paste. Set aside.

Add the fenugreek seeds to the pan and another 1 tablespoon of oil, followed by the chillies, curry leaves and two of the tomatoes, and cook for 10 minutes further, stirring often. Add the curry powder paste, turmeric and chilli powder, and cook for another 10 minutes.

Add the tamarind along with 3 teaspoons of the salt, the sugar and 1 litre (35 fl oz) of hot water, then bring to a simmer. Next, add the coconut milk and simmer for 20–25 minutes. Taste the sauce and check whether you might want to add more salt or sugar.

Bring the sauce to the boil and add the fish, cooking for 3–4 minutes until the fish starts to come to the surface. Use a slotted spoon to check it – it should be totally opaque and starting to flake. When the fish is cooked, add the okra and the last chopped tomato and finally the Roti King spice mix. Take the pan off the heat, add the green chilli and leave the fish to continue to poach for another 3–4 minutes before serving.

NOTE
I like to make it using king fish, but you could swap for any white fish. While I use the whole fish and cut it into chunks, you could chop up fillets if preferred – the firmer the flesh the better, so that it keeps together in the sauce.

KARI AYAM
CHICKEN CURRY

This chicken curry is a favourite on the Roti King menu. We serve this alongside Roti Canai (see pages 35–6), as the sauce is perfect for dipping. You can also swap the chicken for mutton – it works just as well. Add 800g (1lb 2oz) mutton to the pan with the garlic and ginger pastes and curry leaves. Seal the meat until the juices are released, then add 1 litre (35fl oz) of hot water to the pan. Cook this for a further 45 minutes, covered, before adding the dry spices and the coconut to the pan, then cook for a final 10–15 minutes.

SERVES 2–4, AS A SIDE
PREP TIME 5 MINUTES
COOK TIME 15 MINUTES

2 tbsp vegetable oil

2 cardamom pods, bashed

2 star anise

1 cinnamon stick

½ tsp fennel seeds

2 cloves

2 large onions, sliced

2 tsp salt

3 tsp Ginger Paste (see page 138)

1 tsp Garlic Paste (see page 138)

10 curry leaves

½ tsp turmeric powder

2 tsp Roti King Spice Mix (see page 134)

3 tbsp curry powder

1 tsp Kashmiri chilli powder

60g (2¼oz) coconut block

800g (1lb 12oz) skinless boneless chicken thighs, diced into 2–3cm (¾in–1in) pieces

15–20g (½–¾oz) coriander (cilantro), stalks and leaves finely chopped

Heat the oil in a large, lidded, high-sided saucepan set over a medium heat. Add the cardamom pods, star anise, cinnamon stick, fennel seeds and cloves, then fry for 2 minutes to release the aromatics. Add the onion and 1 teaspoon of salt and cook for 6–8 minutes until softened and starting to colour. Add the ginger and garlic pastes along with the curry leaves and cook for 5 minutes, stirring continuously.

Add the turmeric, 1 teaspoon of the Roti King spice mix, curry powder, Kashmiri chilli powder, the remaining teaspoon of salt along with with 50-100ml (1½fl oz– 3½fl oz) of hot water, and cook for 15 minutes, stirring throughout.

Add 500ml (17fl oz) of just-boiled water along with the coconut block and stir to melt the coconut. Once melted, add the chicken thighs, bring to the boil, then turn the heat down to a gentle simmer and cook with the lid on for 25–30 minutes, until the chicken is cooked through. Taste the sauce – you may want to add a little more salt. When you are happy, add the final teaspoon of spice mix, stir to combine and serve with the fresh coriander scattered on top.

KANGKUNG BELACAN
MORNING GLORY AND SHRIMP PASTE

This is a great, strong and punchy side dish to go alongside roti and kari. The addition of simple ingredients like sambal, crispy onions and chilli adds texture and heat, making this one of my favourite ways to eat my greens. Morning glory (also called water spinach) can be found in Asian supermarkets. If you can't get hold of morning glory you can substitute with other green vegetables; try this recipe with green beans, spinach or okra, adjusting the cooking times accordingly.

SERVES 2–4, AS A SIDE
PREP TIME 5 MINUTES
COOK TIME 15 MINUTES

1 tbsp vegetable oil

2 garlic cloves, minced

1 tsp toasted shrimp paste

2 tbsp Basic Sambal (see page 132)

1 tbsp oyster sauce

250g (9oz) morning glory, hard or thicker stalks removed

¼ tsp salt

½ fresh red chilli, stalk removed and finely sliced, to serve (optional)

1 tbsp Crispy Fried Shallots (see page 142 or store-bought)

2 spring onions (scallions), finely sliced (optional)

In a large, lidded frying pan or wok, heat the oil over a low heat. Add the garlic and shrimp paste and cook for 2 minutes (with the lid off), stirring throughout to stop the shrimp paste sticking or the garlic burning.

Add the sambal and oyster sauce and cook for another 5 minutes. Add the morning glory and salt along with 5 tablespoons of water. Cover with a lid and cook for 2–3 minutes until completely wilted. Serve hot topped with the sliced chilli, crispy fried shallots and spring onions, if using.

ROTI KING DAL VG

This is my mum's recipe and I've been cooking it since the early Roti King days. Back when I was selling food from market stalls and kiosks across London, this was a good, tasty dish that I could make with inexpensive ingredients. Now a top seller on the Roti King menu, too, it's delicious served alongside roti.

I recommend using a pressure cooker for this recipe as it uses less water and takes less time.

For those without one, I give instructions for cooking on the stove, whereby the dal is cooked separately to speed things up. If you are doubling up the recipe, remember you may need to add more water and it will take longer to cook. It's important that the split peas are washed properly before cooking – a thorough wash should involve four washes and rinses.

SERVES 4–6
PREP TIME 20 MINUTES
COOK TIME 95 MINUTES

300g (10½oz) yellow split peas, thoroughly washed

1 tsp ground turmeric

4 garlic cloves

1 tbsp vegetable oil or ghee

½ cinnamon stick

2 star anise

½ tsp brown or black mustard seeds

1 large onion, finely diced

1 dried Kashmiri chilli, roughly chopped

12 curry leaves, picked from the stalks

2 tsp Ginger Paste (see page 138)

100g (3½oz) tomatoes, finely chopped

1 tsp salt

2 tbsp sambar powder (or any curry powder, such as garam masala)

15–20g (½–¾oz) coriander (cilantro), stalks and leaves finely chopped

In a large, lidded saucepan, add the split peas, turmeric and garlic along with 2 litres (4¼ pints) of boiling water. Bring to a boil, then reduce the heat to a simmer and cook, covered, for 90 minutes or until the split peas have softened.

In a separate frying pan set over a medium heat, add the oil or ghee and when hot, add the cinnamon, star anise and mustard seeds. Cook for 2 minutes before turning the heat down and adding the onion, chilli and curry leaves. Cook for another 10 minutes until the onions are coloured and soft. Add the ginger paste, tomatoes and salt, and cook for another 10 minutes, then add the sambar spice mix to the pan.

Once the dal has been cooking for 90 minutes, taste it and check the split peas are soft. If it needs longer, continue to cook until soft. Once cooked, add the tomato and onion mixture to the dal, along with the coriander, and stir together. Serve the dal hot with roti.

CHAR KWAY TEOW
STIR-FRIED NOODLES WITH EGG AND PRAWNS

This is a dish of Chinese origin, with 'char' meaning to stir-fry and 'kway teow' referring to the flat noodle that's traditionally used. It's a very popular street-food dish in Singapore and Malaysia, usually served with egg and prawns or chicken. This recipe method reflects how a street-food vendor would cook this in front of you.

SERVES 2
PREP TIME 10 MINUTES
COOK TIME 5–7 MINUTES

3 tbsp vegetable oil

8 prawns (shrimp), preferably shell-on, heads and shells removed

2 garlic cloves, finely chopped

3 eggs, whisked

400g (14oz) cooked thick rice noodles

150g (5½oz) beansprouts

5g (⅛oz) chives, chopped into thirds

2 tsp Crispy Fried Shallots (see page 142 or store-bought), to serve

2 spring onions (scallions), sliced, to serve

For the sauce

2 tbsp Basic Sambal (see page 132)

3 tbsp oyster sauce

3 tsp fish sauce

2 tsp dark soy sauce

1 tbsp light soy sauce

1 tsp chicken powder

1 tsp caster (superfine) sugar

Before you get started, it's important to note that a hot pan is essential here – the food must be cooked over a high heat in order to achieve the best results. It comes together very quickly, so you need to have all the ingredients prepped before you heat the pan, and add them in the exact order in which they appear in the recipe. Have a wooden spoon or spatula ready to move the ingredients around the pan as soon as they're added.

Combine all the sauce ingredients in a small bowl.

Add the oil to a large non-stick frying pan set over a high heat. Add the prawns, stirring for 1 minute before adding the garlic. After 10 seconds, add half the whisked eggs, stir, then add the noodles. About 30 seconds later, add the sauce to the pan, mixing it together well. Add the remaining eggs, the beansprouts and the chives. Pour 3 tablespoons of water into the bowl you used to make the sauce, swirl it around and tip into the pan. Keep stirring everything together – the egg should be cooked and the sauce should have coated everything.

Serve with a scattering of crispy fried shallots and spring onions.

AYAM GORENG BEREMPAH

ROTI KING FRIED CHICKEN

This fried chicken can be served on its own or as part of a bigger meal with lots of other sides. It's also traditionally served as part of Nasi Lemak (see page 52). The marinade in this recipe makes enough for two batches of chicken. I recommend storing the extra in a sterilized jar in the fridge, where it will keep for up to a week, or freezing it. Once you've made this, you will want to eat it again before too long.

SERVES 6
PREP TIME 15 MINUTES, PLUS 1 HOUR–24 HOURS TO MARINATE
COOK TIME 10 MINUTES

40g (1½oz) cornflour (cornstarch)

30g (1oz) rice flour

200ml (7fl oz) vegetable oil, plus more for deep-frying

1.2kg (2lb 7oz) small chicken, skin-on, chopped into 14 or equiavalent cuts of your choice (see note)

10 curry leaves

For the lemak marinade

1 large onion, roughly chopped

3 lemongrass sticks, tops cut off and bottoms bashed and roughly chopped

1 tsp Garlic Paste (see page 138)

2 tsp Ginger Paste (see page 138)

10 lime leaves, stalks removed

10g (¼oz) turmeric

large handful of curry leaves

80ml (2½fl oz) vegetable oil

1 tsp curry powder

2 tsp salt

Add all the marinade ingredients to a blender and blitz to a smooth paste.

Mix half of the marinade with the cornflour, rice flour and vegetable oil. Place the chicken pieces in a large mixing bowl and use your hands to work the marinade all over the chicken. Leave to marinate in a sealed container for a minimum of 1 hour and up to 24 hours in the fridge, before frying.

When you're ready to cook, pour enough vegetable oil into a medium saucepan so that it reaches halfway up. Place it over a medium heat and once the oil reaches 165°C (330°F) fry the chicken in batches for 6–10 minutes, turning carefully with tongs, until golden and crispy. Remove with a slotted spoon and drain on paper towels. Add the curry leaves to the pan for 30 seconds or until crispy, then remove with a slotted spoon and drain on paper towels.

Serve the chicken hot with the crispy curry leaves.

NOTE
If you prefer to avoid having to cut up the chicken, you can buy cuts of your choice, such as legs or thighs. Just be sure to buy skin-on and bone-in, as these add so much flavour. Ensure the pieces of chicken are similar sizes as cooking times may vary.

MAMAK MEE GORENG
FRIED NOODLES WITH TOFU AND PRAWNS

'Mamak' refers to the Indian origins of this dish, while mee means 'noodles' and goreng is 'fried'. This is a dish I tried to learn to cook for a while. Back home in Ipoh there was one particular spot that sold a very good version of this, so to learn the flavours in the hope of recreating this myself, I ate this a lot – at one point a few times a week! I've tweaked it over the years, but I owe this recipe to the man whose version was so good I kept returning to it. And to myself for such commitment to eating my favourite meal until I could make it myself – the best kind of research! The Roti King mee goreng includes chicken and prawns, but here I use just prawns and tofu, which is my favourite variation.

SERVES 2
PREP TIME 10 MINUTES
COOK TIME 5 MINUTES

2 tbsp vegetable oil

6 medium prawns (shrimp), peeled

1 garlic clove, finely chopped

2 eggs

270g (9½oz) cooked egg noodles

2 fried tofu puffs, sliced

large handful of beansprouts

For the sauce

2 tsp dark caramel sauce (see page 22)

2 tsp light soy sauce

2 tbsp oyster sauce

2 tbsp Basic Sambal (see page 132)

½ tsp shrimp paste

1 tsp chicken powder

1 tsp caster (superfine) sugar

3 tbsp roasted peanuts, bashed using a pestle and mortar or finely chopped

Before you get started, it's important to note that a hot pan is essential here – the food must be cooked over a high heat in order to achieve the best results. It comes together very quickly, so you need to have all the ingredients prepped before you heat the pan, and add them in the exact order in which they appear in the recipe. Have a wooden spoon or spatula ready to move the ingredients around the pan as soon as they're added.

In a medium bowl, combine all the ingredients for the sauce.

Heat a large non-stick frying pan over a high heat. Pour in the oil, once hot add the prawns, moving them around the pan quickly, then after 30 seconds–1 minute, once they're pink, move them to the side of the pan and add the garlic. Stir for 10 seconds before moving the garlic to the side of the pan with the prawns as you crack the eggs into the pan. Leave for 10 seconds (as if you are frying the eggs) before stirring them together, breaking them up and mixing with the prawns and garlic. Continue to stir and scrape the bottom of the pan as you go so that it doesn't stick or burn (don't be tempted to turn the heat down). Add the cooked egg noodles, keeping the heat high. Next add the tofu and then immediately pour over the sauce. Mix until everything is well coated and scatter over the beansprouts, stirring for a minute before serving.

NASI LEMAK

COCONUT RICE WITH SPICY SAMBAL AND EXTRAS

Nasi lemak is considered the national dish of Malaysia. It centres around aromatic coconut rice with lots of extra ingredients added for flavour and texture. Peanuts give a delicious crunch, the sambal adds a spicy element, the cucumber is there to cool the spice, the anchovies offer salty umami and the fried chicken and soft-boiled egg add protein to make the meal filling. Each ingredient complements the other, resulting in a brilliant plate of food. In Malaysia it's a dish that can be eaten at any time of day, from breakfast through to the evening.

To make this pescatarian, leave out the fried chicken, or to make it vegetarian, you can also omit the fried anchovies.

SERVES 8–10

These are the components

of Nasi Lemak

Sambal Ikan Bilis (see page 133)

Coconut Rice (see page 108)

dried anchovies (as page 17 or fried with the peanuts, see page 123)

peanuts (as they are or with the fried anchovies, see page 123)

Ayam Goreng Berempah (see page 48)

soft-boiled egg

cucumber slices

This is essentially a collection of the elements that make up Malaysia's famous nasi lemak – read through each of the individual recipes before getting started.

Start by making the sambal – this can sit while you prepare the rest of the elements of the nasi lemak. Once you've made the sambal, you can start the coconut rice and the fried anchovies and peanuts. For the anchovies and peanuts, I suggest following the recipe for Ikan Bilis Kacang Goreng and adding chilli to taste, or you could individually fry dried anchovies and peanuts. You want to make a start on the fried chicken last as it's at its best served hot. The soft-boiled egg and cucumber slices can prepared while the chicken is frying, as they only take a couple of minutes to put together.

RENDANG

Rendang originated in Indonesia before becoming popular across south-east Asia, and now it's particularly associated with Malaysia. It's spicy, sweet and very fragrant, as it includes both lemongrass and lime leaves. I learned how to cook rendang from my mum and my auntie in Seremban. My mum's version uses fresh green chillies, which I have kept in my recipe while also adding dried Kashmiri chillies, giving a darker colour and, in my opinion, a better taste too. As with many Malaysian recipes, this dish begins by preparing the paste, which you can do well in advance, if you wish. My mum taught me to cook the meat separately to the paste but I like to cook them together in one pan for ease. Rendang is not particularly saucy, it's drier than classic karis and is always eaten with rice or roti.

We serve the shiitake mushroom rendang at Roti King with coconut rice. Here I've also given a recipe for chicken rendang, but you can make this with beef or lamb. For lamb, follow the method for the chicken rendang, instead using about 600g (1lb 5oz) of lamb shoulder. For beef, use about 600g (1lb 5oz) of brisket – seal the meat over a high heat before it cooking it separately for about 45 minutes over a low heat and then add it to the pan with the paste.

RENDANG PASTE

MAKES ENOUGH TO MAKE
EACH OF THE RENDANG
RECIPES THAT FOLLOW

2–4 fresh green chillies (depending on your heat preference), stalks removed

5 dried Kashmiri chillies, seeds removed

2 lemongrass sticks, tops cut off and bottoms bashed and roughly chopped

35g (1¼oz) turmeric

35g (1¼oz) galangal (or ginger)

1 tbsp oil

Blitz all of the ingredients along with 100ml (3½fl oz) of water in a blender until it becomes a smooth paste. Add a little more water to loosen, if needed.

If you're not using this straightaway, keep it in an airtight container in the fridge for up to two weeks.

RENDANG AYAM

CHICKEN RENDANG
SERVES 4–6
PREP TIME 10 MINUTES
COOK TIME 50 MINUTES

3 tbsp vegetable oil

1 cinnamon stick

1 lemongrass stick, bashed

1 batch (approx. 500g/1lb 2oz) Rendang Paste (see page 54)

600g (1lb 5oz) chicken thighs, skin-on and bone-in

1½ tsp salt

40g (1½oz) fresh or frozen shredded coconut (see page 16 for preparation), or 60g (2¼oz) coconut block

130ml (4fl oz) coconut milk

2 tsp dark brown sugar

¼ tsp coriander seeds

¼ tsp fennel seeds

6 lime leaves, stems removed, finely sliced into strips

We serve a beef version of this at the Roti King restaurants, but chicken works so well with the aromatic spices that I wanted to include a recipe here. Enjoy it with a steaming bowl of Coconut Rice (see page 108).

Heat the oil in a large lidded pan over a medium heat, break the cinnamon stick in half and add to the pan with the lemongrass. Add the rendang paste and cook for 5–10 minutes over a low heat, stirring often.

Add the chicken along with the salt, give it a good stir, then reduce the heat to low and cover with the lid. Cook for 10 minutes, stirring occasionally.

In a separate non-stick frying pan set over a medium heat, toast the shredded coconut (or coconut block), stirring continuously until it's golden brown – this should take 3 minutes. Remove from the pan and pound to a paste using a pestle and mortar. If you are using coconut block, there is no need to pound as the consistency should already be smooth.

Add 100ml (3½fl oz) of water to the chicken, stir and cover again. Leave to cook for a further 20 minutes, stirring occasionally. Add the coconut milk and cook for another 10 minutes, then add the toasted coconut and the sugar. In a small dry pan, toast the coriander and fennel seeds until fragrant and starting to pop. Remove from the pan and bash roughly using the pestle and mortar. Tip straight into the pan with the chicken.

Add the lime leaves, cook for another 2 minutes and serve.

RENDANG CENDAWAN VG

**PULLED SHIITAKE
MUSHROOM RENDANG
SERVES** 4
PREP TIME 10 MINUTES
COOK TIME 35–40 MINUTES

5 tbsp vegetable oil

1 cinnamon stick

1 lemongrass stick, bashed

1 batch (approx. 500g/1lb 2oz)
  Rendang Paste (see page 54)

800g (1lb 12oz) shiitake, oyster or
  other mushrooms, thinly sliced

1½ tsp salt

40g (1½oz) fresh or frozen
  shredded coconut (see page 16
  for preparation), or 60g (2¼oz)
  coconut block

130ml (4fl oz) coconut milk

2 tsp dark brown sugar

¼ tsp coriander seeds

¼ tsp fennel seeds

6 lime leaves, stems removed,
  finely sliced into strips

Achar Timun, to serve (optional,
  see page 144)

This meat-free rendang is a favourite in the restaurant, and this at-home version uses fresh shiitake and oyster mushrooms for their firm, meaty texture and robust flavour – but any mushrooms will do if you can't find them. The trick to getting the most flavour out of the mushrooms is to allow them to catch slightly in the pan before adding the liquid.

Heat 3 tablespoons of oil in a large lidded pan over a medium heat, break the cinnamon stick in half and add to the pan with the lemongrass. Add the rendang paste and cook for 5–10 minutes over a low heat, stirring often.

Add the mushrooms, 2 tablespoons more oil and 1 teaspoon of salt, give it a good stir, then reduce the heat to medium and cover with the lid. Cook for 10 minutes, stirring occasionally – you want the mushrooms to catch slightly on the bottom of the pan.

In a separate non-stick frying pan set over a medium heat, toast the shredded coconut (or coconut block) until browned and golden, stirring continuously until it's golden brown – this should take 3 minutes. Remove from the pan and pound to a paste using a pestle and mortar. If you are using coconut block, there is no need to pound as the consistency should already be smooth.

Add 100ml (3½fl oz) of water to the mushrooms, stir and cover again. Leave to cook for a further 10 minutes, stirring occasionally. Add the coconut milk and cook for another 10 minutes, then add the toasted coconut and the sugar. In a small dry pan, toast the coriander and fennel seeds until fragrant and starting to pop. Remove from the pan and bash roughly using the pestle and mortar. Tip straight into the pan with the mushrooms.

Add the lime leaves, cook for another 2 minutes and serve with rice and achar timun, if you like.

MEAT & FISH

DAGING DAN IKAN

This chapter includes many favourite family recipes, like the Fish-head Curry (see page 66), that helped put my parents' Ipoh restaurant on the map, alongside other quick meals I like to cook for my family. There are some classic Malaysian recipes, alongside others that are less traditional and make use of store-cupboard ingredients – all with meat or fish as the hero.

TERUNG SARDINE SAMBAL

AUBERGINE AND SARDINE STEW

Aubergine and sardines make an unusual combination in Malaysian cooking, which I've only come across once, at a roadside stall in Buntong, Ipoh. This delicious stew is created from my memory of eating this there. It's quick to prep this one-pan dish, which relies mostly on store-cupboard ingredients – perfect for a weeknight dinner. I use canned sardines in tomato sauce, which you can find in most supermarkets, though it would also work well with canned mackerel. Serve this with rice or roti.

SERVES 4
PREP TIME 5–10 MINUTES
COOK TIME 45 MINUTES

2 tbsp vegetable oil

1 onion, sliced

2 dried Kashmiri chillies

1 tsp Ginger Paste (see page 138)

3 garlic cloves, halved

1 large aubergine (eggplant), cut into 2cm (¾in) chunks

2 medium tomatoes, finely chopped

3 tbsp Basic Sambal (see page 132)

1 tsp tamarind mixed with 2 tbsp warm water, strained

2 x 95g (3½oz) cans sardines in tomato sauce

15g (½oz) coriander (cilantro), leaves picked and roughly chopped

Heat the oil in a large, lidded saucepan over a medium–high heat. Add the onion and fry for 5 minutes, stirring often, before adding the dried chillies and the ginger paste. Fry for 1 minute, stirring continuously, then add the garlic, aubergine, tomatoes and 150ml (5fl oz) of just-boiled water.

Turn the heat down to medium and leave to cook with the lid on for 20 minutes, stirring from time to time. Add the sambal and tamarind, place the lid back on and cook for another 15 minutes.

Check the stew – the aubergine should be soft and starting to lose its shape – and add a splash more water if it's sticking to the bottom of the pan. Add the sardines and their sauce into the pan, mix to combine and cook for a further 5 minutes. Serve with the coriander stirred through, alongside roti or rice.

CRAB KAM HEONG

CHINESE–MALAYSIAN AROMATIC CRAB

This is one of my favourite dishes to make at home for my family and guests and I usually cook the crab in an air fryer, but you can also steam it. More typically found on restaurant menus in Malaysia than at street-food stalls, kam heong is Chinese–Malaysian fusion at its best. In this recipe I use crab, but the sauce also works well with any other seafood as well as chicken, and served with plain or coconut rice alongside. It's messy to eat because you need to use your hands to break the shell, but it's definitely worth it.

SERVES 4–6
PREP TIME 10 MINUTES
COOK TIME 30 MINUTES

2 crabs (see note)

2 tbsp curry powder

3 tbsp vegetable oil

1 onion, finely chopped

2 tbsp Basic Sambal (see page 132)

1 tsp dark caramel sauce (see page 22 or swap for dark soy)

1½ tbsp oyster sauce

1½ tsp salt

1 tsp caster (superfine) sugar

½ tsp chicken powder

4g (⅛oz) dried shrimp, roughly chopped

2 fresh green chillies, stalks removed and finely chopped

3 lemongrass sticks, tops cut off and bottoms bashed and finely chopped

4 garlic cloves, finely chopped

20 curry leaves

Using a steamer, or a large pot with a tight-fitting lid and a metal colander or heatproof bowl, steam the crab pieces for about 10 minutes until cooked – the shell of the crab will change to red once cooked. If not using a steamer, ensure the crabs are not touching the boiling water – you want to steam them (not boil them).

Mix the curry powder with 4 tablespoons of water to form a paste and set aside.

In a large, lidded frying pan heat 1 tablespoon of the oil over a medium–high heat. Fry the onion and sambal for 10 minutes. Add the curry paste and fry for another 5 minutes, while gradually adding 100ml (3½fl oz) of water, a tablespoon at a time, stirring continuously. Once all the water has been added and the sauce has been combined, add the caramel sauce, oyster sauce, salt, sugar and chicken powder, and cook for a further 5 minutes.

In a separate frying pan set over a medium heat, pour in the remaining 2 tablespoons of oil and once hot add the dried shrimp, green chillies, lemongrass, garlic and curry leaves. Fry for 1 minute.

Add the cooked crab into the curry sauce followed by the shrimp mixture. Stir everything to combine before putting the lid on and cooking over a low heat for 5–7 minutes, by which time the sauce should have reduced and become sticky.

NOTE
Ask your fishmonger to break the crab into four pieces, removing the inedible gills.

CAULIFLOWER STIR-FRY WITH PRAWNS

This dish isn't typically Malaysian – it's a simple recipe from my own kitchen that I often make when I need a quick fix. It takes less than 15 minutes to prep and cook. You can serve this stir-fry with rice.

SERVES 2
PREP TIME 5 MINUTES
COOK TIME 8 MINUTES

1 tbsp vegetable oil

2 garlic cloves, finely chopped

1 small cauliflower, cut finely into small florets

1 carrot, peeled and sliced into thin rounds

8 king prawns (shrimp), shelled

½ tsp salt

¼ tsp ground white pepper

2 tbsp oyster sauce

2 spring onions (scallions), chopped into 2cm (¾in) lengths

Heat the oil in a large, lidded pan set over a medium heat. Add the garlic and cook for 2 minutes, stirring continuously. Add the cauliflower and carrot and cook for another 4 minutes. Add the prawns and stir to combine, before adding the salt, white pepper, oyster sauce and 5 tablespoons of water.

Increase the heat to medium–high and cook with the lid on for 4 minutes. Add the spring onions to the pan, stir to combine and serve.

TAUGEH IKAN MASIN

BEANSPROUTS WITH TOFU AND SALTED FISH

This dish is cooked fast over a high heat so it's really important to have all the ingredients prepared before you start cooking. Remember to add the beansprouts to the pan just for a short time so that they retain some crunch. You can buy salted fish from larger supermarkets – be sure to buy skinless and boneless.

SERVES 4
PREP TIME 5–10 MINUTES
COOK TIME 8 MINUTES

2 tbsp vegetable oil

3 garlic cloves, minced

1 piece of skinless and boneless salted fish (about 25g/¾oz), finely chopped (I use Cawoods)

small handful of chives, chopped into 2cm (¾in) lengths

2 fried tofu puffs, finely sliced

300g (10½oz) beansprouts

1 tsp fish sauce

1 tbsp oyster sauce

2 tbsp Crispy Fried Shallots (see page 142 or store-bought)

2 spring onions (scallions), finely sliced

Heat the oil in a large frying pan over a high heat. Add the garlic, fish, chives and tofu, and cook over a high heat for 2–3 minutes, stirring continuously.

Add the beansprouts and stir together before adding the fish sauce and oyster sauce. Stir to combine before removing from the pan and serving immediately, topped with crispy fried shallots and spring onions.

KARI KEPALA IKAN

PADMA'S FISH-HEAD CURRY

This was originally my grandmother's recipe, who passed it down to my mum. It became the signature dish that made our restaurant, Gopal's Corner, in Ipoh, so popular. When my parents first started serving this, fish heads were free from their local market, where my dad would pick them up for my mum to cook. It's because of my dad that they started charging for fish heads – at first it was 20p per head but now it's more like £15! Ask your fishmonger for the head of a large fish such as a red snapper or garupa/grouper. Or you could use four small salmon heads. Serve with rice. Any leftover sauce is really delicious with poached eggs as a snack (see page 124).

SERVES 4
PREP TIME 10 MINUTES
COOK TIME 45 MINUTES

100g (3½oz) fish curry powder or regular curry powder

3 tbsp vegetable oil

5 prawn (shrimp) shells and heads – the leftover prawn shells from Prawn Sambal (see page 75) or Char Kway Teow (see page 47) can be saved to make this curry

150g (5½oz) tamarind, mixed with 600ml (20fl oz) warm water, strained

200g (7oz) coconut milk

1 tsp fenugreek seeds

1 onion, finely sliced

15 curry leaves

5 tsp salt

1 tbsp caster (superfine) sugar

1 fish head (approx. 2kg/4lb 8oz), halved

2 large tomatoes, quartered

5 okra, topped and tailed

2 fresh green chillies, stalks removed and halved

Start by mixing the curry powder with 100ml (3½fl oz) of water in a small bowl until a ball forms, then set to one side.

Add all the paste ingredients (see ingredients list opposite) to a blender and blitz to a smooth paste.

In a large, lidded saucepan over a medium heat, add 1 tablespoon of the oil, and once hot fry the prawn shells and heads for 3 minutes, stirring often. Add 1 litre (35fl oz) of water and bring to a rolling boil. After 10 minutes take the pan off the heat, strain the water (reserving it) to remove the shells, discarding them. Pour the water back into the pan and place over a medium heat, add the curry powder paste along with the strained tamarind and coconut milk and mix together. Take the pan off the heat and put to one side.

Meanwhile, add the remaining 2 tablespoons of oil to a frying pan set over a low heat. Add the lemongrass and garlic paste and fry for 5 minutes. Add the fenugreek, sliced onion and curry leaves, and fry for a further 7 minutes until the onions are softened. Add this mixture into the sauce, followed by the salt and sugar and stir well. Bring to the boil and add the fish head halves, followed by the tomatoes, okra and green chillies. Turn the heat down to medium–low and cover the pan, cooking for 6 minutes before turning the fish head over and cooking for a further 6 minutes. This cooking time will depend on the size of the fish head – you'll know the fish is cooked when the eyes become opaque. If the eyes are still translucent the fish needs longer.

NOTE
The paste for this recipe calls for a whole bulb of garlic to be blitzed with the skin on, which is a trick used to help mask the smell of the fish heads (the fragrant lemongrass helps with this too).

For the paste

3 lemongrass sticks, tops cut off
and bottoms bashed and
roughly chopped

1 whole garlic bulb (unpeeled),
cloves separated (see note)

1 tbsp cumin seeds

1 tsp black peppercorns

PADMA'S TIGER PRAWNS

This isn't a traditional recipe, but it's something my mum always cooked for big occasions at home, like Diwali. Often with Diwali, we spend at least three days eating lots of delicious meat-based dishes and so my family love to make this when people are coming over for something a little different. We usually serve it with rice.

SERVES 2–4
PREP TIME 15 MINUTES
COOK TIME 40 MINUTES

2 tbsp vegetable oil

4 tsp salt

1 tsp soft dark brown sugar

20g (¾oz) tamarind mixed with 70ml (2¼fl oz) warm water, strained

6 large tiger prawns (shrimp), shell on

10g (¼oz) coriander (cilantro), leaves picked

For the paste

2 tbsp vegetable oil

2 onions, roughly chopped

1 lemongrass stick, bashed and roughly chopped

10g (¼oz) ginger, roughly chopped

5 fresh red chillies, stalks removed and roughly chopped

4 garlic cloves, halved

½ tsp coriander seeds

½ tsp cumin seeds

½ tsp white poppy seeds

40g (1½oz) fresh or frozen shredded coconut (see page 16 for preparation)

½ tsp shrimp paste

First make the paste. Heat 2 tablespoons of the oil in a large, lidded frying pan set over a medium heat. Add the onions, lemongrass, ginger, chillies and garlic, and cook for 3 minutes, stirring regularly. Move these ingredients to the side of the pan, reduce the heat to low and add the coriander, cumin and poppy seeds along with the coconut, and cook for 1 minute. Add the shrimp paste and cook for a further 3 minutes.

Take the pan off the heat before transferring to a blender along with 150ml (5fl oz) of cold water and blitzing to a smooth paste.

Add the remaining 2 tablespoons of oil into the same pan and place it over a medium heat. Add the paste and fry for 8 minutes or until cooked out as per the instructions on page 25. Add 450ml (15fl oz) of just-boiled water to the pan and cook for a further 10 minutes. Add the salt, sugar and tamarind, then cook for a further 3 minutes, stirring continuously. The sauce should now be thick – add the prawns, cover with the lid and cook for 5 minutes before turning the prawns over and cooking for a further 5 minutes. Scatter with the fresh coriander leaves and serve.

SATAY

CHICKEN OR LAMB AND PEANUT SAUCE

Inherited from Indonesian cuisine, satay refers to any meat marinated and cooked on sticks – think of it as south-east Asia's version of the kebab, commonly a dish cooked over charcoal at roadside stalls. This recipe makes more marinade than needed for either the chicken or the lamb, but the extra keeps well in a jar in the fridge for up to three weeks or frozen in portions for up to six months. For best results, marinate the meat overnight. You'll need bamboo skewers for this recipe – soak these overnight. The sauce is served alongside for dipping.

MAKES 10 SKEWERS
PREP TIME 10 MINUTES
PLUS 4 HOURS MARINATING
COOK TIME 30 MINUTES

350g (12oz) chicken thighs,
  boneless, skin-on, chopped into
  chunky strips

OR

400g (14oz) small lamb cutlets

100g (3½oz) marinade (see below)

For the marinade

4 lemongrass sticks, tops cut off
  and bottoms bashed and roughly
  chopped

30g (1oz) galangal, peeled

30g (1oz) turmeric

3 tsp salt

1 tsp Kashmiri chilli powder

4 tbsp dark brown sugar

5 tbsp vegetable oil

10g (¼oz) ginger

1 tsp ground coriander

1 tsp ground cumin

Add the marinade ingredients to a blender and blitz to a paste. Place the meat in a large dish or ziplock bag and pour over the marinade, ensuring the meat is completely covered. Transfer to the fridge and leave to marinate for 4 hours or overnight.

Combine all the glaze ingredients in a small bowl and set aside.

To make the satay sauce, start by making a paste by blending the galangal, ginger, coriander, cumin, dried chillies and shallots with 50ml (1½fl oz) of water, and mix together. Heat the oil in a medium pan over a high heat and add the paste along with the salt, then cook for 8–10 minutes, stirring continuously. Add the peanuts and 250ml (8½fl oz) of hot water to the pan, and stir to combine. Add the brown sugar, coconut milk, pandan leaf and tamarind and cook for a further 10 minutes over a medium heat.

When you are ready to cook the meat you'll need a hot charcoal grill. Brush the meat with the glaze before cooking and thread the chicken strips on to pre-soaked bamboo skewers. Cook the chicken for 4–5 minutes on each side or until cooked through and the lamb for 2–4 minutes on each side or until cooked through.

Serve the chicken or lamb with the satay, either drizzled over or on the side.

For the glaze

3 tbsp caster (superfine) sugar

1 tsp salt

2 lemongrass stalks, bashed

1 tsp oil

1 red chilli, halved

250ml (8½fl oz) boiling water

For the satay sauce

10g (¼oz) galangal

10g (¼oz) ginger

¼ tsp ground coriander

¼ tsp ground cumin

4–6 dried Kashmiri chillies
(depending on your spice
preference), stalks removed

85g (3oz) shallots, roughly chopped

4 tbsp vegetable oil

2 tsp salt

200g (7oz) toasted peanuts,
crushed

2 tbsp soft brown sugar

50ml (1½fl oz) coconut milk

1 fresh pandan leaf, tied in a knot

1 tsp tamarind mixed with 50ml
(1½fl oz) warm water, strained

西饼屋
埔鷄飯

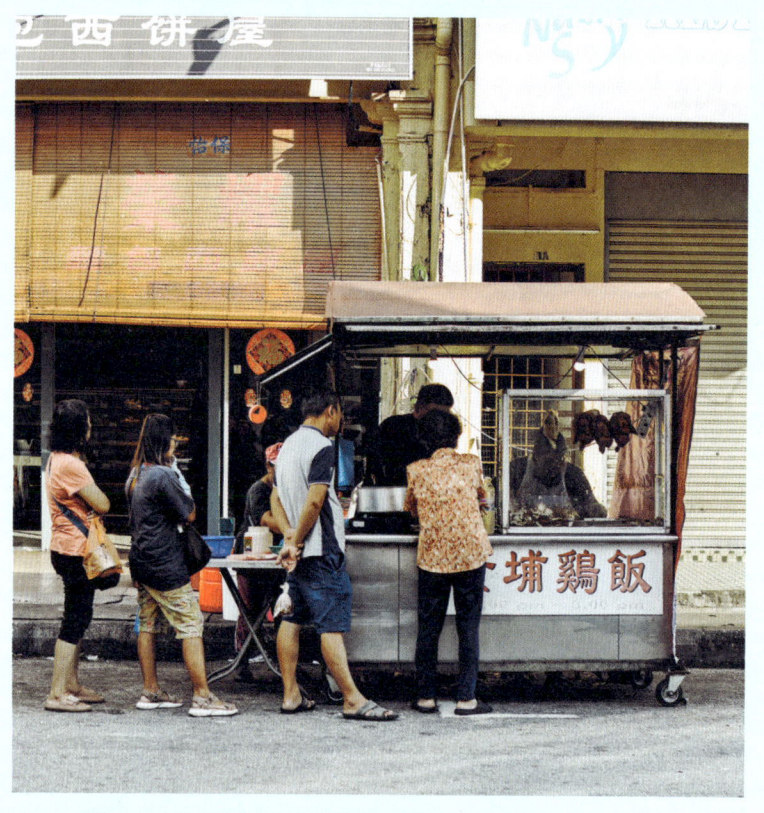

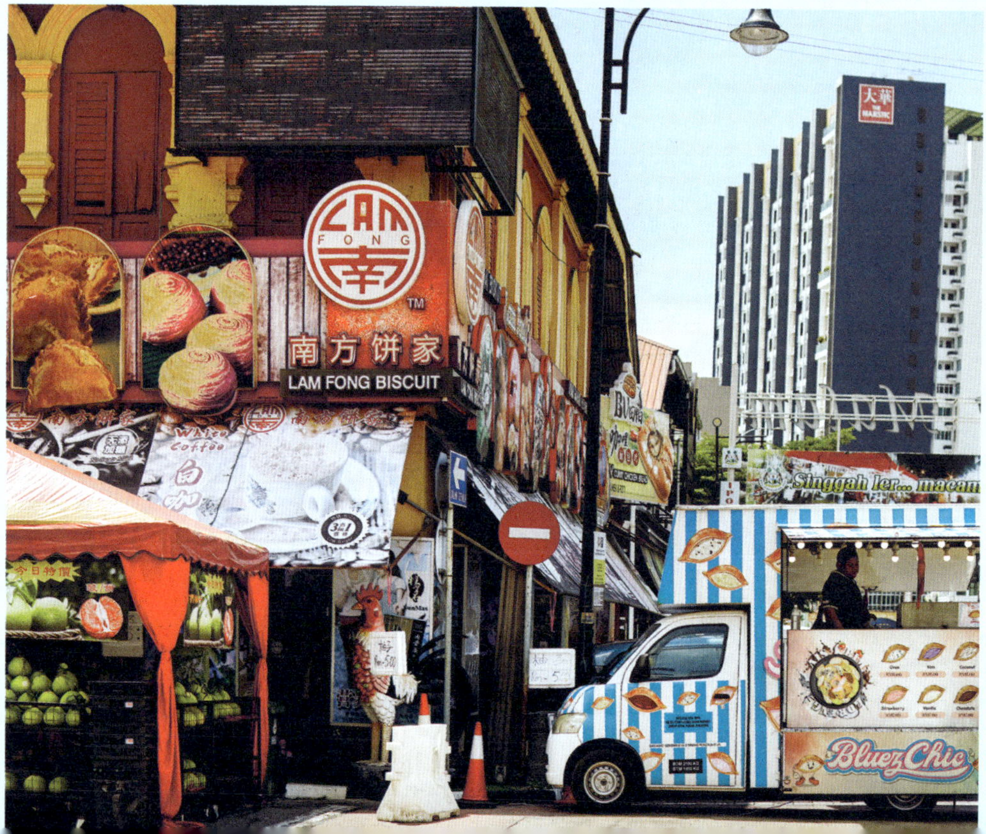
LAM FONG
TM
南方饼家
LAM FONG BISCUIT
今日特價
Singgah ler... macam
BluezChic

ASAM PEDAS
SOUR AND SPICY FISH

For this recipe, the most important ingredient is the torch flower as it adds such a nice aromatic flavour to the fish. You can use fresh or frozen for this recipe, though fresh is always better. It's not the easiest ingredient to find – I often bring it back from Malaysia with me, but you can find it online or try asking in your nearest Asian supermarket.

SERVES 4–6
PREP TIME 10 MINUTES
COOK TIME 35 MINUTES

2 tbsp vegetable oil

200g (7oz) tamarind mixed with 100ml (3½fl oz) warm water, strained

15g (½oz) salt

2 tsp caster (superfine) sugar

2 sea bass fillets (approx. 180g/6oz), skin-on, each chopped into 4–5 chunks

1 large tomato, sliced into 6 wedges

100g (3½oz) okra, topped and tailed

3 lime leaves

5g (⅛oz) coriander (cilantro), leaves and stalks roughly chopped

For the paste

2 garlic cloves

20g (¾oz) ginger

5g (⅛oz) fresh or frozen torch flower (see recipe introduction)

½ tsp Kashmiri chilli powder

½ tsp ground turmeric

5g (⅛oz) shrimp paste

1 lemongrass stick, bashed and roughly chopped

3 lime leaves

3 shallots, roughly chopped

3 fresh red chillies, stalks removed

Add all of the ingredients for the paste along with 200ml (7fl oz) of water to a blender and blitz until smooth.

Add the oil to a large saucepan set over a medium–high heat. Once hot, add the paste and cook for 10 minutes, stirring often. Pour 100ml (3½fl oz) of hot water into the pan and cook for a further 15 minutes.

Add the tamarind to the pan, along with the salt and sugar. Stir well and cook for a further 2 minutes. Reduce the heat to low and add the fish, tomato and okra, and cook for 5 minutes. Tear the lime leaves into halves and add to the pan, remove from the heat and stir to combine. Serve topped with coriander.

SUP AYAM
CHICKEN SOUP

This is a deliciously light soup with warming aromatics. Sup ayam is particularly popular in the rainy season in Malaysia, usually served by street vendors with a baguette alongside. The potato collapses to thicken the soup and the chicken poaches in the flavoursome broth to make a very simple and comforting meal.

SERVES 2
PREP TIME 5 MINUTES
COOK TIME 45 MINUTES

1 tbsp vegetable oil

2 star anise

2 cloves

1 cinnamon stick

2 tsp Ginger Paste (see page 138)

1 small potato, peeled and cut into 2cm (¾in) chunks

1 carrot, peeled and cut into 1cm (½in) chunks

450g (1lb) chicken thighs, skin-on, bone-in

½ tsp ground turmeric

1 tsp chicken powder

1 tsp cumin seeds

1 tsp white pepper

1 tsp ground coriander

2 tsp salt

½ tsp ground black pepper

3 medium tomatoes, finely sliced

2 spring onions (scallions), finely sliced, to serve

2 tbsp Crispy Fried Shallots (see page 142 or store-bought), to serve

bread, to serve

Pour the oil into a large, lidded saucepan and set over a medium heat. Once hot, add the star anise, cloves and cinnamon followed by the ginger paste, then stir for 1 minute before adding 1 litre (35fl oz) of hot water and bringing to the boil. Add the potato and the carrot, reduce the heat and simmer for 10 minutes. Add the chicken along with the turmeric, chicken powder, cumin seeds, white pepper, coriander, salt, black pepper and the tomatoes. Cover with a lid and cook for a further 25 minutes.

Add 300ml (10½fl oz) of boiling water and cook for a further 10 minutes with the lid off. The soup is ready when the chicken is falling off the bone, the potatoes are collapsing and the carrot is tender. Scatter with the spring onions and crispy fried shallots, and serve with bread for dipping.

SAMBAL UDANG

PRAWN SAMBAL

This prawn sambal is deliciously spicy and simple to make and pairs nicely with the Coconut Rice (see page 108). You could even use this sambal for the Nasi Lemak (see page 52).

SERVES 4–6
PREP TIME 5 MINUTES
COOK TIME 25 MINUTES

3 tbsp vegetable oil

2 onions, finely sliced

450g (1lb) king prawns (shrimp), shells on

1½ tsp salt

1 tbsp tamarind mixed with 2 tbsp warm water, strained

10g (¼oz) coriander (cilantro), leaves picked and finely chopped

For the paste

10 fresh red chillies, stalks removed

2 lemongrass sticks, tops cut off and bottoms bashed and roughly chopped

1 tsp Ginger Paste (see page 138)

1 tsp Garlic Paste (see page 138)

1 tsp shrimp paste

Add all of the ingredients for the paste to a blender along with 100ml (3½fl oz) of water and blitz until completely smooth.

In a large frying pan over a medium heat, add the oil. Once hot, add the onions and cook, stirring often, for 8–10 minutes until softening. Move the onions to the side of the pan and add the prawns to the other side and fry until pink, turning them over to ensure they're cooked on both sides before removing from the pan (leaving the onions as they are) and setting aside.

Add the paste to the pan with the onions along with the salt. Cook for 2 minutes, stirring continuously, before pouring in 150ml (5fl oz) of boiling water. Fry for another 8 minutes to cook the paste out, then add the tamarind.

Add the prawns back to the pan, stir and cook for a final 3 minutes, adding 1–2 tablespoons more water if the sauce needs to loosen. Serve topped with the chopped coriander.

IPOH KUEY TEOW SOUP
IPOH-STYLE PRAWN CHICKEN NOODLE SOUP

The best beansprouts in the world are thought to hail from my hometown, Ipoh, and this recipe brings together another ingredient for which the city is famous – poached chicken. This soup is the first dish I seek out when I return there, as I love the tender poached chicken, crunchy fresh beansprouts and the delicious aromatic broth. I give directions to cook the broth for 60 minutes minimum – don't skip or speed up this part of the recipe as the broth needs this time for the flavours to develop. I use fresh noodles here, but you could use dried, just prepare according to packet instructions.

SERVES 4
PREP TIME 10 MINUTES
COOK TIME 1 HOUR
20 MINUTES

450g (1lb) chicken thighs, skin-on, bone-in

10 king prawns (shrimp), heads and shells on

1 tbsp vegetable oil

2 tsp salt

1 tsp chicken powder

½ tsp white pepper

400g (14oz) fresh flat rice noodles

200g (7oz) beansprouts

10g (¼oz) chives, chopped into 2cm (¾in) lengths

1 tbsp sesame oil

1 tbsp soy sauce

1 clove garlic, finely chopped

2 bird's eye chillies, finely sliced

2 tbsp Crispy Fried Shallots and oil (see page 142 or store-bought)

Start by bringing 2 litres (4¼ pints) of water to the boil in a large saucepan or stockpot. Once boiling, add the chicken, reduce the heat to medium and simmer for 15 minutes, covered. Keeping the pan of water on the heat, remove the chicken thighs and immediately plunge them into a bowl of iced water. The ice-cold water will cool the chicken quickly, ensuring it doesn't overcook, and keeps the texture tender. After 5 minutes, drain the chicken and refrigerate while you prepare the rest of the soup.

Remove the shells and heads from the prawns and return the prawns to the fridge. In a small frying pan, heat the oil over a medium heat, fry the heads and shells for 3 minutes, then remove from the pan to cool. Transfer the shells and oil from the pan to a blender and blitz, before adding them to the water, along with the salt, chicken powder and white pepper. Cook the broth for a minimum of 60 minutes, letting it simmer over a medium heat – once you start to see the water reduce, add 500ml (17fl oz) more boiling water.

Strain the broth and return the liquid to the pan, placing it back over a medium heat. Add the prawns, cooking for 2 minutes until pink, then remove from the pan with a slotted spoon. Set them aside to cool, then slice in half lengthways.

Add the noodles to the broth, cooking for 1 minute to heat them through. Remove and divide between serving bowls. Add the beansprouts and chives to the pan to cook for 1 minute, then remove and divide between the bowls. Add the poached chicken thighs to the pan, simmering for 5 minutes. Using a meat probe, check the chicken has reached 75°C (167°F), then remove it and slice up before adding to the bowls on top of the noodles and veg. Pour a drizzle of sesame oil on top of the chicken. Divide the halved prawns between the bowls and ladle the hot broth over the top.

In a small bowl, add the soy sauce, garlic and chillies and mix. Set aside.

Scatter the noodle bowls with the crispy fried shallots and shallot oil, and serve piping hot with the soy sauce and finely chopped fresh chillies on the side, if you like.

IKAN MASAK CILI KERING

DRIED CHILLI-GINGER FISH

This dish was inspired by a chicken dish that I first tried in Ipoh, in a restaurant that has since sadly closed down. When I came to the UK, I wanted to try to make a version using cod, which is much more readily available here than in Malaysia. The meaty texture of the fish stands up well to the sweet, spicy sauce. I like to serve this family-style, with rice and a side of Kangkung Belacan (see page 43).

SERVES 4
PREP TIME 10 MINUTES
COOK TIME 30 MINUTES

2 tsp cornflour (cornstarch)

1 tbsp butter

500g (1lb 2oz) cod fillets, skin-on and chopped into 3cm (1in) chunks

1 tsp white pepper

3 tbsp vegetable oil

½ tsp Garlic Paste (see page 138)

1 tbsp Ginger Paste (see page 138)

½ tsp chicken powder

½ tsp dark brown soft sugar

1 tbsp oyster sauce

2 tsp dark caramel sauce (see page 22)

2 tbsp Chinese cooking wine

3 round shallots, cut into thirds

5g (⅛oz) ginger, sliced into matchsticks

10 whole dried Kashmiri chillies, stalks removed and roughly chopped

4 spring onions (scallions), halved lengthways

2 tbsp Crispy Fried Shallots (see page 142 or store-bought) and oil, to serve

In a small bowl, mix the cornflour with 3 tablespoons of water to form a paste, then put to one side.

Heat a large frying pan over a medium heat. Add the butter, and once melted add the cod with ½ teaspoon of the white pepper. Fry for 5 minutes, stirring to make sure the fish is cooked and starting to brown, then remove from the pan and set aside.

Add 2 tablespoons of the vegetable oil into the same pan. Once hot, add the garlic and ginger pastes, cook for 30 seconds, then add 300ml (10½fl oz) of boiling water and cook for 5 minutes over a high heat, stirring often. Add the remaining ½ teaspoon of white pepper along with the chicken powder, sugar, oyster sauce and caramel sauce. Mix in the cornflour paste and continue to stir until you have a thick sauce. Turn the heat down to medium, add the fish back into the pan along with the wine and cook for another 5 minutes.

Meanwhile, in another small frying pan, add the remaining 1 tablespoon of oil and place over a medium heat. Fry the shallots, ginger, dried chillies and spring onions for 5 minutes, stirring often. Add this mixture into the pan with the fish, stir to combine and serve immediately with crispy fried shallots and oil to garnish.

MASAK LEMAK CILI API
SPICY COCONUT MACKEREL

This curry calls for turmeric leaf, an ingredient often used in recipes from southern India. If you can't get hold of it, substitute it with lime leaves. Dried bean curd (tofu) stick is also used in this recipe, if you can't get that, just leave it out of the recipe, or use fresh. This sauce works really well with prawns (shrimp), too. Serve with rice and roti or you can even stir through rice vermicelli noodles for the last few minutes.

SERVES 4
PREP TIME 10 MINUTES
COOK TIME 30 MINUTES

1 dried tofu stick

2 tbsp vegetable oil

2 lemongrass sticks, tops cut off, bottoms bashed

3 tsp salt

½ small white cabbage (about 120g/4¼oz), shredded

1 small tomato, diced

200ml (7fl oz) coconut milk

2 medium mackerel fillets, skin-on, sliced into thirds

100g baby spinach leaves

1 tsp tamarind mixed with 1 tbsp warm water, strained

For the paste

5g (⅛oz) turmeric leaf or 3 lime leaves, stem removed

2 garlic cloves

2 green bird's eye chillies

2 red bird's eye chillies

10g (¼oz) turmeric

1 onion, roughly chopped

1 tsp dried shrimp

Add all the paste ingredients into a blender along with 250ml (9fl oz) of water and blitz until smooth.

Soak the tofu in a small bowl of just-boiled water for 5–10 minutes and put to one side.

Heat the oil in a large frying pan over a medium heat, add the paste and lemongrass. Cook for 5–7 minutes, stirring often, until the oil starts to separate from the paste. Add the salt, followed by the cabbage, tomato, coconut milk and 100ml (3½fl oz) water, and cook for another 5 minutes. Drain the tofu stick and add to the pan, along with the mackerel, and cook for 10 minutes with the lid on. Then add the spinach and cook for a further 5 minutes before adding the tamarind and serving.

CHICKEN MASALA

The paste used in this recipe is one of my mum's, which she always uses as a base for Padma's Tiger Prawns (see page 69). Here I use it for chicken, with a few tweaks to her paste, and it's my favourite version. Serve with coconut rice or any of the rotis, if you like (see pages 108 and 35–38).

SERVES 4
PREP TIME 10 MINUTES
COOK TIME 1 HOUR
10 MINUTES

1 tbsp vegetable oil

½ cinnamon stick

2 star anise

1 tsp Kashmiri chilli powder

1 tsp paprika

70g (2½oz) cherry tomatoes, finely sliced

600g (1lb 5oz) chicken thighs, skin-on and bone-in

2 tsp salt

30ml (1fl oz) coconut milk

1 tbsp dried pandan leaves, roughly chopped

2 tbsp Roti King Spice Mix (see page 134)

1 tsp soft dark brown sugar

10g (¼oz) coriander (cilantro), leaves picked and roughly chopped

First make the paste (see list opposite). Heat the oil in a large, lidded saucepan over a medium heat. Add the onions and cook for 10 minutes, stirring throughout. Add the rest of the paste ingredients and cook for a further 3 minutes before adding 100ml (3½fl oz) of water, stirring to combine. Leave to cool for 10 minutes before decanting into a blender and blitzing to a smooth paste.

Pour the oil into the same pan and add the cinnamon and star anise, then cook for 1 minute to toast the spices. Add the paste, the chilli powder and paprika and cook over a medium–high heat for 6–7 minutes, stirring often. Stir in the tomatoes, then add the chicken, salt and 100ml (3½fl oz) of water. Stir, cover with the lid and cook for 20 minutes. Add the coconut milk and cook, covered, for another 10 minutes. Add the pandan leaves and 1 tablespoon of the Roti King spice mix and the sugar, and cook, uncovered, for a further 10 minutes over a low heat. Serve with the remaining spice mix and the coriander leaves scattered over.

For the paste

3 tbsp vegetable oil

3 onions, roughly chopped

1 lemongrass stick, bashed and
  roughly chopped

4 garlic cloves

2 tsp Ginger Paste (see page 138)

5 fresh red chillies, stalks removed
  and roughly chopped

25g (1oz) fresh or frozen shredded
  coconut (see page 16 for
  preparation)

1½ tsp fennel seeds

1½ tsp coriander seeds

½ tsp cumin seeds

½ tsp white poppy seeds

IKAN BAKAR SUMBAT

FILLED BARBECUED FISH

This popular dish is comprised of fish wrapped in a banana leaf, served with a spicy sauce. In Malaysia, it's often sold at night markets, where you can pick the fish from a selection, have it filled with a paste of your choice and barbecued to order. Traditionally it's cooked over a charcoal fire before being wrapped in a banana leaf, where it slowly steams, meaning the skin is crispy and the fish inside remains deliciously tender.

For cooking this at home, I give options to barbecue, bake or pan-fry the fish. Each method uses a banana leaf to wrap the fish. The filling in this recipe is inspired by Thai flavours and I use mackerel, though it works well with any other small fish. Serve this with rice and a simple green salad, with the sauce alongside.

SERVES 4
PREP TIME 10 MINUTES
PLUS 2 HOURS MARINATING
COOK TIME 30 MINUTES

2 whole mackerel, gutted and descaled

3 tbsp Basic Sambal (see page 132)

2 tbsp tom yum paste

For the filling

1 tsp dried shrimp

2 fresh red chillies, stalks removed

1 tsp lime juice

1 tbsp fresh or frozen shredded coconut (see page 16 for preparation)

1 shallot, roughly chopped

1 lemongrass stick, bashed

1 tsp salt

Add the filling ingredients to a blender and blitz to a paste. Fill each fish with half of this mixture and place on a baking sheet.

Mix together the sambal and tom yum paste, and pour it over the fish. Leave to marinate, covered in the fridge for a minimum of 2 hours.

Combine all the sauce ingredients (see list opposite) in a small bowl.

The fish can be cooked on a barbecue, in a pan or in the oven. Each method aims to cook the fish on both sides until the skin is crispy, before wrapping the fish tightly in a banana leaf (see opposite), and returning to your method of cooking (barbecue, oven or frying pan) to steam the fish and continue cooking.

To barbecue, first cook the fish on the lowest heat for 3–4 minutes on each side (timings will vary depending on your barbecue), before wrapping the fish in the banana leaf and cooking on a higher heat until cooked. The fish should look opaque but still tender.

If using the oven, preheat it to 220°C/200°C fan/425°F/gas 7 and cook for 15 minutes wrapped in the banana leaf.

To pan-fry, heat a non-stick frying pan over a high heat, lay the banana leaf out onto the pan and cook the fish for 4 minutes on each side, until the skin is crispy. Then wrap the fish in the banana leaf and cook for 1 more minute to steam the fish before removing from the pan.

Serve with rice and the sauce alongside.

For the sauce

1 shallot, finely diced

2 fresh red chillies, stalks removed
   and finely diced

1 medium tomato, seeds removed
   and finely diced

1 tbsp tamarind mixed with 100ml
   (3½fl oz) water, juice strained

1 tbsp fish sauce

15g (½oz) coriander (cilantro),
   stalks and leaves finely chopped

AYAM MASAK MERAH
RED CHICKEN

In Malaysia, this is a special-occasion dish, something often eaten at weddings and other celebrations. Serve alongside the Tomato Rice (see page 109) with the Achar Timun (see page 144), if you like.

SERVES 4–6
PREP TIME 15 MINUTES
COOK TIME 40 MINUTES,
PLUS 30 MINUTES
MARINATING

1 whole chicken (approx. 1½kg/3lb 5oz), cut into 12 parts (see note)

2 tsp Kashmiri chilli powder

1 tsp ground turmeric

1 tsp Garlic Paste (see page 138)

1 tsp Ginger Paste (see page 138)

1 tsp salt

vegetable oil, to shallow-fry

1 cinnamon stick

2 cardamom pods

1 star anise

2 cloves

2 onions, finely sliced

2 tsp salt

1½ tbsp tomato purée (paste)

3 tbsp tomato ketchup

1 fresh pandan leaf

1 tbsp dark brown sugar

10g (¼oz) coriander (cilantro), leaves picked and roughly chopped

Add all the paste ingredients (see list opposite) to a blender with 100ml (3½fl oz) of water and blitz until smooth.

Place the chicken parts in a large dish and add the chilli powder, turmeric, garlic paste, ginger paste and salt, then massage them into the meat. Leave to marinate for 30 minutes in a sealed container at room temperature.

Fill a large frying pan with 1cm (½in) of oil and place over a high heat. Once hot, add the chicken pieces and fry for 5 minutes on each side until the chicken is crispy and coloured (depending on your pan size you may need to do this in batches). Remove the chicken with tongs or a slotted spoon and put to one side. Remove the oil from the pan, decanting it into a heatproof bowl or jug, then put to one side.

In a larger, high-sided, lidded frying pan or wok, add 6 tablespoons of the reserved oil and, once hot, add the cinnamon, cardamom, star anise and cloves. Fry the aromatics for 1 minute before adding the onions and cook for a further 5 minutes until starting to soften (but without colouring). Add the paste and cook for 10–15 minutes, stirring often until it's bubbling and starting to separate. Add the salt, tomato purée, ketchup and the pandan leaf. Add 6 tablespoons of water along with the sugar, then continue to cook the sauce for 5 minutes. Add the chicken into the pan, put the lid on and cook over a low heat for another 10 minutes. Serve hot scattered with the coriander.

NOTE
If you prefer to avoid having to cut up the chicken, you can buy cuts of your choice, such as legs or thighs. Just be sure to buy skin-on and bone-in, as these add so much flavour. Ensure the pieces of chicken are similar sizes as cooking times may vary.

For the paste

10g (¼oz) dried Kashmiri chillies

3 fresh red chillies, stalks removed

3 lemongrass sticks, white parts
 only, bashed and roughly chopped

100g (3½oz) galangal

2 onions, roughly chopped

1 small tomato, roughly chopped

THAI-STYLE BAKED SEA BASS

This oven-baked sea bass is such a simple recipe to feed a crowd and is an impressive dish to serve at the table. Ask your fishmonger to descale, gut and butterfly your fish for you, and amend the cooking times if you have a smaller or larger fish. Coriander root is often used in Thai cooking and can be found in Asian supermarkets, but if you can't get hold of it, replace it with coriander stalks.

SERVES 4
PREP TIME 15 MINUTES
COOK TIME 30 MINUTES

2 lemongrass sticks, tops cut off and bottoms bashed and finely chopped

30g (1oz) coriander root, finely chopped

3 fresh red chillies, stalks removed and finely chopped

3 garlic cloves, finely chopped

120ml (4½fl oz) lemon juice

120ml (4½fl oz) fish sauce

90g (3oz) brown sugar

1 large sea bass, approx. 900g (2lb), skin-on, descaled, gutted and butterflied (see recipe introduction)

20g (¾oz) ginger, finely sliced into matchsticks

10g (¼oz) coriander (cilantro), leaves and stalks, to serve

Preheat the oven to 200°C/180°C fan/400°F/gas 6.

Add the lemongrass, coriander root, chillies and garlic to a bowl with the lemon juice, fish sauce and brown sugar. Mix to combine and leave this to one side to start to pickle while you prepare the sea bass.

Place the fish in a high-sided baking dish, skin side up, top with the ginger and bake in the oven for 25 minutes. Remove the dish from the oven, pour over most of the sauce, covering the whole of the fish, and bake for a further 5 minutes.

Serve the fish whole to the table on a platter or in the baking dish topped with the coriander, with the remaining sauce on the side.

HAINANESE CHICKEN RICE

Brought to Malaysia from China from the island of Hainan, in the South China Sea, this dish is popular across Malaysia and Singapore and is one of the more well-known dishes in this book. This is one of those clever recipes that makes the most of the whole chicken, the flavours of the bird helping to produce the most fragrant rice and broth.

The most important part of this recipe is the poached chicken, which must be cooked over a low heat to ensure it is tender and juicy. As with the Ipoh soup on page 76, it is really important that the meat is cooked perfectly. The flavours of the poached chicken are very delicate, but paired with the punchy chilli sauce, Hainanese chicken rice ticks all the boxes.

SERVES 6
PREP TIME 10 MINUTES
COOK TIME 90 MINUTES

For the chicken

1 whole chicken, approx. 1.6kg (3½lb)

15g (½oz) ginger, skin-on, sliced

For the chilli paste

8 fresh red chillies, stalks removed, half deseeded

5g (⅛oz) ginger

50ml (1½fl oz) malt vinegar

2 tsp caster (superfine) sugar

2 tbsp salt

For the rice

2 tsp butter

1 tsp Ginger Paste (see page 138)

2 fresh pandan leaves

750g (1½lb) long grain rice, washed thoroughly and drained

1 tsp salt

2 tbsp chicken powder

¼ tsp ground turmeric

In a large saucepan that will comfortably fit the chicken, place the chicken and enough water to completely submerge the bird. This will depend on the size of the pot but should be around 6 litres (12½ pints). Add the skin-on ginger to the pan. Bring the water up to the boil and then simmer for 20 minutes with the lid on. Remove the lidded pot from the heat, turn the chicken over and leave submerged for 15 minutes. Check the chicken is cooked by inserting a knife into one of the breasts – the juices should run clear. If not, simply poach for a further 5 minutes. Remove the chicken from the pan and place in iced water. Discard the ginger.

Put the large saucepan back on the heat with the lid on and again bring to the boil, then simmer for 40 minutes.

Add all the chilli paste ingredients to a blender and blitz until smooth.

Meanwhile, prepare the rice. In another large saucepan over a medium heat, melt the butter. Add the ginger paste and pandan leaves and toast for a minute. Stir through the rice to coat the grains for another minute. Add 1.4 litres (3 pints) of the chicken stock from the pan along with the salt, chicken powder and turmeric. Bring to the boil, then turn down to a simmer and cook as per the packet instructions of the rice, with the lid on.

Combine the sauce ingredients in a pan on a medium heat for 5 minutes.

Remove the chicken from the ice bath. Debone the thighs, wings, drumsticks and breasts – keep the the skin on the breasts and slice the meat, as pictured opposite.

Slice the cucumber in angular wedges, then place on a large plate or platter with the rice and neatly sliced chicken breasts. Pour over the sauce and scatter with the crispy fried shallots and some oil, sesame oil and chopped spring onion.

For the chicken sauce

800ml (1½ pints) chicken stock (prepared from the whole chicken)

1 tsp chicken powder

1 tsp dark caramel (see page 22)

2 tsp oyster sauce

1 tbsp light soy sauce

1 tbsp Chinese wine

1 tbsp dark brown sugar

¼ tsp Chinese five spice

15g (½oz) coriander (cilantro), leaves picked

To serve

½ cucumber, thickly sliced

2 tbsp Crispy Fried Shallots and oil (see page 142 or store-bought)

1 tbsp sesame oil

4 spring onions (scallions), finely sliced

VEGETABLES & SIDES

SAYUR–SAYURAN

Usually when eating together as a family or for a celebration, lots of main dishes would be served alongside vegetables and side dishes. It's rare that there wouldn't be a large selection of side dishes served, with plenty of rice, of course. You'll find stir-fries, salads, stews and everything in between in this chapter. Lots of these dishes are influenced by friends and family, while others are more street-food style.

RASAM VG

TOMATO GARLIC BROTH

This is the dish I crave when I'm feeling under the weather or run down, as I find it gives me a boost. It's packed full of garlic (renowned for helping to fight infection), which is blitzed to a paste with the skins on. This soup is also considered to be very good for digestion, so in Malaysia it's often served at the end of a meal.

SERVES 4
PREP TIME 10 MINUTES
COOK TIME 15 MINUTES

½ tsp ground turmeric

2 tsp salt

10 curry leaves

10g (¼oz) coriander (cilantro), stalks and leaves roughly chopped, plus extra to serve

50g (1¾oz) tamarind mixed with 100ml (3½fl oz) water, strained

For the paste

10 garlic cloves, unpeeled

2 medium tomatoes

2 tsp freshly ground or whole black peppercorns

2 tsp cumin seeds

2 tsp coriander seeds

1 dried Kashmiri chilli

50g (1¾oz) cherry tomatoes, roughly chopped

First make the paste by adding all the ingredients apart from the cherry tomatoes into a blender along with 100ml (3½fl oz) of water. Blitz to a smooth paste. Add the cherry tomatoes and pulse to combine.

In a medium–large saucepan, bring 800ml (1¾ pints) of water to the boil along with the turmeric and the salt. Once boiling, add the paste, curry leaves and coriander, and simmer for 5 minutes. Stir through the tamarind juice and serve piping hot with an extra scattering of coriander.

IPOH PUMPKIN STEW VG

This is my mum's recipe that we serve in Gopal's Corner. Traditionally a festival food for times of feasting, it would appear along with lots of other vegetable dishes, served alongside meat and fish. This flavour-packed stew makes a great autumnal dinner when squash and pumpkins are in season. Any variety can be used for this recipe – if using butternut squash, I like to keep the skin on, but you may want to peel other varieties with tougher skins.

SERVES 4–6
PREP TIME 10 MINUTES
COOK TIME 30 MINUTES

2 tbsp vegetable oil

2 cardamom pods, bashed

½ tsp brown mustard seeds

½ cinnamon stick

2 cloves

½ tsp fennel seeds

¼ tsp fenugreek

1 large onion, roughly chopped

2 tsp salt, plus ½ tsp more,
    if needed

1 dried Kashmiri chilli, roughly
    chopped

5g (⅛oz) curry leaves

1 tsp Ginger Paste (see page 138)

1 tsp Garlic Paste (see page 138)

1 medium tomato, roughly chopped

½ tsp ground turmeric

2 tsp Kashmiri chilli powder

3 tsp caster (superfine) sugar, plus
    ½ tsp more, if needed

900g (2lb) butternut squash or
    pumpkin, diced into 2cm (¾in)
    chunks

1 tbsp tamarind mixed with 2 tbsp
    warm water, strained

Heat the oil in a large, lidded, high-sided saucepan set over a medium heat. Add the cardamom pods, mustard seeds, cinnamon, cloves, fennel seeds and fenugreek, then fry for 2 minutes to release the aromatics.

Add the onion and cook for 5–6 minutes until softened but not coloured. Add 1 teaspoon of the salt, the dried chilli and the curry leaves and stir together. Add the ginger paste, stir to combine, then add the garlic paste and tomato, and continue to stir for 1 minute. Add the turmeric, chilli powder, the remaining teaspoon of salt and the sugar, followed by the squash or pumpkin. Add 300ml (10½fl oz) of hot water, put the lid on the pan and lower the heat. Leave to simmer for 20 minutes, stirring from time to time.

After 20 minutes, use a fork to test if the squash or pumpkin is softening. Taste the sauce – you may want to add half a teaspoon more salt or sugar. Add the tamarind, stir, then take the pan off the heat, leaving it to rest for 5 minutes before serving.

SPINACH DAL VG

This is the quickest dal to make. The yellow moong (often labeled 'mung') dal is the split version of the green moong bean. Don't confuse moong dal with yellow split peas (used in the Roti King Dal on page 45) or the toor dal (used in the Sambar on page 111), which has a much longer cooking time. Here I give instructions for cooking the dal on the stove, but it also works well in a pressure cooker if you have one.

SERVES 4
PREP TIME 10 MINUTES
COOK TIME 35 MINUTES

100g (3½oz) moong dal

100g potato, roughly cubed

1 fresh green chilli, halved
  lengthways

2 whole garlic cloves

1 small shallot, sliced

¼ tsp ground turmeric

1 tbsp vegetable oil

1 onion, finely chopped

¼ tsp black mustard seeds

1 dried Kashmiri chilli, roughly
  chopped

1 tsp Garlic Paste (see page 138)

1 medium tomato, finely chopped

10 curry leaves

120g (4¼oz) baby spinach leaves

1–2 tsp salt

In a medium, lidded saucepan set over a medium–high heat, add the dal, potato, green chilli, garlic, shallot and turmeric. Pour over 700ml (23½fl oz) of hot water and cook, with the lid on, for 20–30 minutes. It's ready when the dal is soft and the potato is easily mashable with a fork.

Meanwhile, heat a medium, high-sided sauté pan over a medium heat. Add the oil and once hot, follow with the onion and cook for 5 minutes until starting to soften. Add the mustard seeds, dried chilli, garlic paste, tomato and curry leaves and cook for a further 10 minutes.

Once the dal is cooked, combine with the onion mixture along with 500ml (17fl oz) of hot water and the spinach. Stir to wilt the spinach, and season with the salt. Serve immediately.

SAMBAL TELUR ^v

EGG SAMBAL

In Malaysia, 'economy rice' stalls can be found in most hawker centres where street-food vendors sell simple dishes at very low price points. Egg sambal, often served alongside cheaper rice dishes, is a go-to dish at such stalls. This recipe is a delicious way to spice up your eggs and can be eaten as a quick snack or a substantial breakfast or lunch served with rice. When I don't have much in my fridge, this is the dish I make.

SERVES 2
PREP TIME 5 MINUTES
COOK TIME 15 MINUTES

4 eggs

2 tbsp vegetable oil

1 onion, finely sliced

2 tbsp Basic Sambal (see page 132)

1 tsp salt

1 tbsp tomato ketchup

1 tsp caster (superfine) sugar

Bring a small saucepan of water to a rolling boil, add the eggs and cook for 10 minutes until they're hard-boiled. Remove, then leave to cool before peeling.

Heat the oil in a frying pan over a medium heat. Add the onions and cook, stirring regularly, for 5 minutes. Add the sambal and continue to cook for another 5 minutes.

Add 150ml (5fl oz) of water to the onions along with the salt and cook for a further 2 minutes before adding the ketchup and sugar. Taste to check you're happy with the sweet–salty balance. Add the boiled eggs to the sambal and cook for a further 2 minutes until everything is hot. Divide the eggs between two plates and eat immediately.

BROCCOLI AND CASHEW STIR-FRY

This side dish comes together extremely quickly and would make a great accompaniment to most meals – I honestly think it would work well alongside all of the recipes in this chapter. This was first made for me by my friend Vasugi. Here, I use Tenderstem broccoli, but you could easily swap it out for other seasonal green vegetables, such as purple sprouting broccoli, asparagus or green beans. The butter is browned slightly, which gives the whole dish a nutty flavour, further amplified by the toasted cashews.

SERVES 4
PREP TIME 10 MINUTES
COOK TIME 10 MINUTES

300g (10½oz) Tenderstem broccoli

2 tsp salted butter

50g (1¾oz) cashews, roughly chopped

2 garlic cloves, finely chopped

2 tsp oyster sauce

2 tbsp Crispy Fried Shallots (see page 142 or store-bought), to serve

Start by blanching the broccoli in a pan of boiling water for 2 minutes, then drain and plunge into ice-cold water. Leave to drain in a colander.

Melt the butter in large pan over a medium heat, and once bubbling, add the cashews and then the garlic. Stir frequently and cook until the butter is just starting to brown. Transfer the garlic and cashew mixture to a plate, before adding the drained broccoli to the pan, keeping it over a medium heat. Add the oyster sauce, and fry for 2–3 minutes until the broccoli has started to soften a little (but being careful not to overcook).

Add the garlic and nuts back into the pan, stir together and serve garnished with the crispy fried shallots.

JELATAH TIMUN NENAS VG

PINEAPPLE AND CUCUMBER SALAD

There aren't many traditional Malaysian salads, especially not ones served by roadside stalls. So, this salad is special and often served at special occasions, such as weddings or festivals like Diwali, where we'd eat it alongside a meal of many different curries and dals. You'll see I've included this salad in the banana leaf meal on page 169 because it works so well as a cooling and refreshing complement to rich, spicy curries.

SERVES 2–4
PREP TIME 10 MINUTES

150g (5½oz) fresh pineapple, sliced into thin wedges

1–2 green chillies, stalks removed and sliced

½ cucumber, peeled and finely sliced into rounds

1 onion, very finely sliced

100ml (3½fl oz) coconut milk

½ tsp salt

15g (½oz) coriander (cilantro), leaves picked, roughly chopped, to serve

Add the pineapple, chillies, cucumber rounds and onions to a large bowl. In a small bowl or jug, mix together the coconut milk and salt with 2 tablespoons of water. Pour this dressing over the fruit and vegetables, making sure everything is completely coated in the dressing before scattering over the coriander.

VARUVAL CRISPY POTATOES

These roast baby potatoes are inspired by South Indian cuisine. Crushing the potatoes this way and roasting them with the spice mix is delicious. The parmesan as an extra topping is great if you are eating these on their own – I got this tip from my teenage daughter, Reathi – but if you are serving these potatoes alongside other dishes you may want to omit the parmesan topping.

SERVES 4
PREP TIME 5–10 MINUTES
COOK TIME 40 MINUTES

500g (1lb 2oz) baby new potatoes

1½ tsp salt

1 tsp Kashmiri chilli powder

1 tsp paprika

1 tsp garlic powder

2 tbsp Roti King Spice Mix (see page 134)

2 tbsp vegetable oil

To serve

5g (⅛oz) coriander (cilantro), leaves picked and roughly chopped

2 tbsp parmesan cheese, finely grated (optional)

pinch of flaky sea salt

Preheat the oven to 220°C/200°C fan/425°F/gas 7.

Tip the potatoes into a large pan of cold water and add ½ teaspoon of the salt. Bring to the boil, then parboil until they are partially cooked – as soon as a fork glides through the potato, they are ready. Drain and leave to steam. Once they're cool enough to handle, tip the potatoes onto a medium-sized flat baking sheet lined with parchment paper. Use the palm of your hand or a flat-bottomed glass to gently crush the potatoes.

In a bowl, mix the chilli powder, paprika, garlic powder, spice mix and 1 teaspoon of salt with 3 tablespoons of water, then pour in the oil. Stir well before pouring over the crushed potatoes, covering each one as best you can. Roast in the oven for 30–35 minutes, turning halfway, until crispy.

Scatter over the coriander, grated parmesan (if using) and a sprinkle of flaky salt before serving.

COCONUT RICE VG

This aromatic rice can be used instead of plain steamed rice and served alongside most meat, fish or vegetable main courses. Use this recipe to make Nasi Lemak (see page 52).

SERVES 6–8
PREP TIME 5 MINUTES
COOK TIME APPROX.
10 MINUTES

500g (1lb 2oz) long grain white rice, washed thoroughly and drained

20g (¾oz) ginger, bashed

1½ tsp salt

400ml (14fl oz) coconut milk

2–3 fresh pandan leaves, tied in a knot

Once you have thoroughly washed the rice, leave it to soak in a bowl with 250ml (9fl oz) of water for 25 minutes.

Drain the rice, add to a rice cooker or large pan with 500ml (17fl oz) of water along with the rest of the ingredients and cook the rice as per the packet instructions.

NASI TOMATO v

TOMATO RICE

This fragrant rice dish can be eaten alongside most curries but it works wonderfully served with Ayam Masak Merah Chicken (see page 86).

SERVES 6–8
PREP TIME 5 MINUTES
COOK TIME 45 MINUTES

500g (1lb 2oz) basmati rice, washed thoroughly and drained

2 tbsp ghee

50g (1¾oz) cashews

50g (1¾oz) raisins

3 cardamom pods

1 star anise

½ cinnamon stick

¼ tsp cumin seeds

1 onion, finely diced

1 tsp Garlic Paste (see page 138)

1 tsp Ginger Paste (see page 138)

5 medium tomatoes, finely sliced

1 lemongrass stick, bashed and halved

2 green chillies, halved

2 tsp salt

10g (¼oz) mint, leaves picked

Once you have thoroughly washed the rice, leave it to soak in a bowl with 250ml (9fl oz) of water for 25 minutes.

Meanwhile, heat a large saucepan over a medium heat. Add the ghee and once hot, add the cashews and raisins and toast for 2 minutes. Once toasted, remove from the pan and set to one side.

Return the pan to the heat and toast the cardamom, star anise, cinnamon and cumin seeds for 2 minutes in the residual ghee. Add the onion and cook for 8–10 minutes until softened and golden, stirring often to prevent any sticking. Add the garlic and ginger pastes and the tomatoes. Cook down for a further 10 minutes or until the tomatoes have collapsed into a sauce.

Drain the rice, add to a rice cooker or large pan with 500ml (17fl oz) of water and the tomato paste. Add the lemongrass stick, chillies, cashews and raisins to the rice, add salt, scatter over the mint and cook the rice as per the packet instructions.

BUNTONG KACANG PANJANG VG
BUNTONG GREEN BEANS

This is a traditional recipe from Buntong, the region of Ipoh where I'm from, which is always served with a banana leaf meal (see page 169).

SERVES 4–6
PREP TIME 5 MINUTES
COOK TIME 10–15 MINUTES

2 tbsp vegetable oil

½ cinnamon stick

¼ tsp cumin seeds

1 red onion, sliced

75g (2½oz) cherry tomatoes, finely chopped

1 dried red chilli, roughly chopped

1 tsp Kashmiri chilli powder

2 tbsp Garlic Paste (see page 138)

10 curry leaves

500g (1lb 2oz) green beans, topped and tailed

3 tbsp fresh or frozen shredded coconut (see page 16 for preparation)

2 tsp salt

Heat the oil in a large frying pan over a medium–high heat. Add the cinnamon and cumin seeds, then after 2 minutes, add the onion and cook for 5 minutes. Stir often to avoid any sticking or burning on the bottom of the pan.

Next, add the tomatoes, stir to soften, then add the dried chilli, chilli powder, garlic paste and curry leaves. Cook for a further 5 minutes until you have a sticky sauce.

Add the green beans along with 3 tablespoons of water. Mix everything well to ensure the green beans are completely coated in the tomato sauce. Add the coconut along with the salt and an extra dash of water if you think the sauce needs loosening. Cook for another 4–5 minutes until the beans are softening. Taste the beans – they are ready when they have softened but still retain a little crunch.

SAMBAR v

SOUTH INDIAN LENTIL AND VEGETABLE STEW

This is a delicious mixed vegetable and lentil stew from South India. It takes longer to cook than many of the recipes in this book, but there's little work to do once you've prepared the vegetables, after which the pot can quietly simmer away. The 'temper' technique of heating the aromatics in hot ghee is used here to intensify their flavour before adding to the dal just before serving. You can make this recipe either on the stove or in a pressure cooker.

SERVES 4 –6
PREP TIME 15 MINUTES
COOK TIME 1–1 HOUR 30 MINUTES

110g (4oz) red split lentils, thoroughly rinsed

110g (4oz) mung dal, thoroughly rinsed

3 garlic cloves

¾ tsp ground turmeric

½ tsp cumin seeds

6 shallots, 3 halved and 3 finely sliced

2 potatoes, peeled and chopped into 2cm (¾in) chunks

1 small aubergine (eggplant), chopped into 2cm (¾in) chunks

2 medium tomatoes, sliced

1 carrot, peeled and chopped into 2cm (¾in) chunks

100g (3½oz) daikon radish, chopped into 2cm (¾in) rounds

100g (3½oz) moringa drumstick, roughly chopped

4 tsp salt

1 tbsp tamarind mixed with 2 tbsp warm water, strained

small bunch of coriander (cilantro), roughly chopped

For the temper

1 tbsp ghee

1 small cinnamon stick

2 cardamom pods

½ tsp black mustard seeds

2 onions, finely chopped

2 dried red chillies, roughly chopped

10 curry leaves

1 tbsp sambar powder

¼ tsp asafoetida powder

In a large, lidded saucepan set over a medium–high heat, add the washed lentils and dal and 500ml (17fl oz) of water. Once simmering, add the garlic, turmeric, cumin seeds and the halved shallots. Add another 2.5 litres (5¼ pints) of hot water, bring the pan to the boil then turn down to a simmer, cooking for 1 hour with the lid on, stirring occasionally.

Add the potatoes, aubergine, tomatoes, carrot, radish, sliced shallots and moringa drumstick and cook for 15 minutes, uncovered, on a gentle simmer, stirring often.

Meanwhile, make your temper. In a small frying pan over a medium–high heat, add the ghee and once melted, add the rest of the temper ingredients, cooking for 4–6 minutes, stirring often. Add the temper into the pan of dal along with the salt, then stir. Add the tamarind juice to the sambar and stir to combine. Serve with a scattering of coriander.

BEETROOT STIR-FRY WITH COCONUT AND PEANUTS VG

In Malaysia, we eat a lot of greens, beans and okra but not a big variety of other vegetables (at least that's my experience!). So, in a bid to eat more vegetables since moving to England, I've started making quick and simple vegetable side dishes to go alongside curries. Beetroot (beets) have a fantastic colour and boast a wealth of health-giving properties. I really like their earthy flavour teamed with the spices here, and the crunch from the peanuts adds texture. The exact cooking time depends on how fresh the beetroot is, but the dish comes together quickly.

SERVES 4
PREP TIME 5 MINUTES
COOK TIME 20 MINUTES

1 tbsp vegetable oil

400g (14oz) fresh beetroot (beets), peeled and diced into 1cm (½in) cubes

1 onion, finely diced

1 tomato, diced

½ tsp black mustard seeds

1 tsp Kashmiri chilli powder

50g (1¾oz) fresh or frozen shredded coconut (see page 16 for preparation)

1 tsp salt

40g (1½oz) roasted peanuts, bashed using a pestle and mortar

Heat the oil in a large frying pan over a medium heat. Add the beetroot, onion and tomato and cook for 10 minutes. Add the mustard seeds and chilli powder along with 3 tablespoons of hot water, then cook for another 10–15 minutes, before adding the coconut and salt.

Check that the beetroot is cooked – it doesn't need to be completely soft but a knife should be able to easily cut through. If the beetroot is too firm, cook for a little longer, adding a splash more water, if needed, and half the peanuts. When the stir-fry is ready, sprinkle over the remaining peanuts and serve.

CABBAGE PORIYAL VG

In Malaysia, this is often served at weddings and special occasions as part of a spread. It was my auntie Indra who taught me this dish and it's now a favourite at Gopal's Corner in London. I like to serve this with dal and rice and it also goes well with the Ipoh Pumpkin Stew (see page 97).

SERVES 4
PREP TIME 10 MINUTES
COOK TIME 25 MINUTES

2 tbsp vegetable oil

1 tsp black mustard seeds

1 onion, finely sliced

2 tbsp yellow split peas

1 dried Kashmiri chilli, roughly chopped

1 tsp Garlic Paste (see page 138)

10 curry leaves

500g (1lb 2oz) cabbage, finely shredded

2 carrots, peeled and julienned or sliced into matchsticks

½ tsp ground turmeric

1 tsp salt

For the coconut paste

15g (½oz) fresh or frozen shredded coconut (see page 16 for preparation)

15g (½oz) ginger, finely chopped

1 green chilli, stalk removed, roughly chopped

½ tsp cumin seeds

First make the coconut paste by combining all the ingredients and using a pestle and mortar or a blender to blitz to a rough consistency.

Pour the oil into a large saucepan set over a medium–high heat, and once hot, add the mustard seeds and the onion. Cook for 5 minutes before stirring through the split peas.

Add the chilli and garlic paste, then stir through the coconut paste. Mix together and cook for 2 minutes, stirring continuously, before adding the curry leaves and the cabbage to the pan. Add 150ml (5fl oz) of water and stir together. Add the carrot, turmeric and salt and cook for a further 15 minutes until the cabbage has softened and the split peas are also soft but still holding their shape.

SNACKS

MAKANAN RINGAN

Malaysians have a loose concept of mealtimes and tend to eat more often than three times a day. A typical day will include lots of snacks, sweet and savoury, picked up from street vendors, which keep us going throughout the day. These sorts of snacks aren't the type of thing you would usually cook at home in Malaysia; instead they're eaten while on the move. Coming up are some of my favourite snack memories adapted into recipes you can cook for a crowd. Some are traditional snacks I grew up eating and others are my creations. I particularly love the Sambal Ikan Bilis Croissant (see page 127), which is both sweet and savoury, and very delicious – a combination I came up with since moving to London, where croissants are readily available.

HATI AYAM MASAK PEDAS
SPICY FRIED CHICKEN LIVER

This is a popular snack, often eaten alongside an alcoholic drink. It's traditionally served on coconut plantations with a toddy – a low-alcohol drink produced by tapping coconut buds before they flower. The liquid is collected overnight, with the producers climbing to the tops of the trees in the morning to collect the sap before leaving the liquid to ferment throughout the day. The flavour and consistency of toddy changes over the course of the day, going from sweet and light to sour and thick. At home, spicy fried chicken liver is served in a banana leaf alongside toddy for the workers of the coconut plantation and visitors. I have fond memories of this delicious snack; I really love it, but I usually skip the toddy! Chicken livers are an inexpensive cut that hold a lot of nutritious value. For this recipe, they need to be marinated for a minimum of two hours for the best results and if you wanted to get ahead, you could leave them to marinate overnight.

SERVES 4
PREP TIME 5 MINUTES,
PLUS 2 HOURS MARINATING
COOK TIME 15 MINUTES

400g (14oz) chicken livers

2 tsp Kashmiri chilli powder

1 tsp curry powder

2 tsp salt

1½ tsp Garlic Paste (see page 138)

1 tbsp lemon juice

3 tbsp vegetable oil

1 onion, finely chopped

¼ tsp cumin seeds

10 curry leaves

4 fresh green chillies, finely chopped

50g (1¾oz) fresh or frozen shredded coconut (see page 16 for preparation)

15g (½oz) coriander (cilantro), roughly chopped

2 tsp Roti King Spice Mix (see page 134)

2 tbsp Crispy Fried Shallots (see page 142 or store-bought), to serve

Start by mixing the chicken livers with the chilli powder, curry powder, salt, garlic paste and lemon juice, and leave to marinate in the fridge, covered, for a minimum of 2 hours or overnight.

When you're ready to cook, heat a large frying pan over a medium heat and add the oil. Once hot, add the onion and fry for 3–4 minutes, stirring often, until starting to soften. Add the cumin seeds, curry leaves and the green chillies, and cook for a further 5 minutes before turning the heat down and adding the livers. Fry for 10 minutes, stirring constantly to keep the liver from sticking to the bottom of the pan. Finely chop the shredded coconut, add this along with half of the coriander and the spice mix, and cook for a further 3 minutes.

Serve immediately topped with the remaining coriander and crispy fried shallots.

CUCUR UDANG

PRAWN AND VEGETABLE FRITTERS

These fritters come together quickly and can be adapted to use any vegetables you have to hand. The batter keeps well for up to two days in a sealed container in the fridge if you want to make it ahead or cook half at a time. The fritters go brilliantly with a dipping sauce, like sweet chilli sauce or the satay sauce on page 70–71.

SERVES 18–20 FRITTERS
PREP TIME 5 MINUTES
COOK TIME 10 MINUTES

5g (⅛oz) dried Kashmiri chilli, finely chopped

10g (¼oz) dried shrimp, finely chopped

2 small garlic cloves, finely chopped

150g (5½oz) king prawns (shrimp), shelled and sliced in half

1 carrot, peeled and cut into matchsticks

1 shallot, finely sliced

150g (5½oz) plain (all-purpose) flour

150g (5½oz) self-raising (self-rising) flour

½ tsp ground turmeric

1½ tsp salt

2 tbsp roughly chopped chives

vegetable oil, for frying

In a large mixing bowl, combine the chilli, dried shrimp, garlic and prawns with 50ml (1½fl oz) of water. Add the carrot and the shallot, and mix together thoroughly. Add both flours along with the turmeric, salt and chives, and mix together. Measure out 300ml (10½fl oz) of water in a jug and slowly pour it into the bowl, stirring the batter as you go – it should be a loose but scoopable consistency.

In a medium frying pan, pour in enough oil to fill it to about 3cm (1¼in) deep. If you have a temperature probe, heat the oil to 180°C (350°F), otherwise test with a small bit of batter – it should sizzle in the oil, float to the surface and start to colour within 30 seconds. Once hot enough, add a generous teaspoon of mixture to the oil and fry each fritter for 90 seconds on both sides until golden. You'll need to fry in batches so as not to overcrowd the pan.

When the fritters are cooked, remove them from the oil with a slotted spoon and place on paper towels to drain. The fritters are delicious served hot or at room temperature. If you want to serve them hot all at once, place them in a low oven (around 170°C/150°C fan/325°F/gas 3) for 5–7 minutes.

IKAN BILIS KACANG GORENG

CRISPY ANCHOVIES AND PEANUTS

This is a really simple snack that is more a combination of good ingredients thrown together in a pan than a proper recipe. It's sometimes served on top of rice dishes, but I prefer it as a pre-dinner snack alongside a drink. The fried anchovies are already salted before they're dried, so I don't add any extra to this recipe, though feel free to do so if you want a saltier taste. I like to eat these warm from the pan, but you can also leave them to cool completely and transfer them to an airtight jar, where they'll stay crispy and delicious for up to a month.

SERVES 4–6
PREP TIME 5 MINUTES
COOK TIME 8–10 MINUTES

250ml (8½fl oz) vegetable oil

150g (5½oz) peanuts, skin-on

10 red bird's eye chillies, finely sliced

75g (2½oz) dried anchovies

15g (½oz) Crispy Fried Shallots (see page 142 or store-bought)

Heat the oil in a medium frying pan over a medium–high heat. Once the oil reaches 170°C (325°F), turn the heat to low, add the peanuts and fry for 4–5 minutes until browned. Remove from the oil with a slotted spoon and place on paper towels in a single layer. Add the sliced chilli to the oil and fry for 30 seconds before removing and placing on paper towels.

Next, add the anchovies to the oil and cook for 3–4 minutes until lightly golden. Remove from the pan with a slotted spoon and place on fresh paper towels to drain the excess oil. When drained, add the peanuts, chillies, crispy anchovies and some crispy fried shallots into a bowl and stir to combine.

LEFTOVER CURRY WITH POACHED EGGS

This is a great way to use up the leftover sauce from my parents' famous Fish-head Curry (see page 66). I think the sauce tastes better the next day and I love to poach eggs in it as a snack or a light breakfast. This recipe is for one person but can be scaled up depending on how much of the curry sauce you have.

SERVES 1
PREP TIME 5 MINUTES
COOK TIME 10 MINUTES

leftover Fish-head Curry sauce (see page 66)

2 eggs

10g (¼oz) coriander (cilantro), leaves picked and roughly chopped

1 Roti (see page 35), to serve (optional)

In a small, lidded frying pan set over a medium heat, add the leftover curry sauce and top up with a little hot water so that the pan is two-thirds full.

Once the sauce is bubbling, carefully crack the eggs into the pan, one at a time, and pop the lid on. Reduce the heat to low and leave the eggs, undisturbed, until they're cooked through to your preferred consistency. Carefully check the eggs with your finger to see if they're ready – I like mine fudgey, which takes around 7–8 minutes.

Scoop into a bowl to serve. Top with the coriander and a roti, if using, to scoop up the sauce.

PRAWN OMELETTE

This is a great dish to make for a light lunch as it's full of protein and flavour. You could make this a more substantial meal by serving it alongside rice, or you could use it to fill a sandwich.

SERVES 2
PREP TIME 5 MINUTES
COOK TIME 5 MINUTES

¼ tsp oyster sauce

¼ tsp white pepper

¼ tsp chicken powder

3 eggs, whisked

8 prawns (shrimp), shells removed, roughly chopped

2 garlic cloves, finely chopped

3 spring onions (scallions), finely sliced

15g (½oz) coriander (cilantro), leaves picked and roughly chopped

1 tbsp vegetable oil

In a medium bowl, mix together the oyster sauce, white pepper, chicken powder and whisked eggs. Add the prawns along with the garlic and two-thirds of the spring onions and coriander.

Heat a medium, lidded frying pan over a medium heat. Add the oil and, once hot, pour in the egg mixture and swirl the pan. Pop the lid on and cook for 3 minutes before flipping over and cooking for a further 2 minutes on the other side. Serve folded on a plate and top with the remaining coriander and spring onion.

SAMBAL IKAN BILIS CROISSANT

I haven't come across this being sold anywhere but it has become one of my favourite homemade snacks and it's especially quick to throw together if you have leftover Sambal Ikan Bilis (see page 133). Use any type of plain croissant and fill it with as much sambal as you can handle. The thick-cut cucumber cools down the chilli heat of the sambal. In Malaysia, we often use cucumber for this purpose, and I think it works particularly well in a sandwich, where it adds texture and a refreshing crunch.

SERVES 1
PREP TIME 5 MINUTES

1 plain croissant

2 tbsp Sambal Ikan Bilis (see page 133)

2 thick slices of cucumber

Slice the croissant in half. Heat a frying pan or griddle over a medium heat and toast the croissant, then remove it from the pan. Spread the sambal on the base. Place the cucumber slices on top and sandwich together with the top of the croissant.

CONGEE

SAVOURY PORRIDGE

In Malaysia, congee is the ultimate comfort food for when you're under the weather, or you just need something warming to eat. There are many different ways to make congee, and in Buntong Market it's often served with chicken or pork, but this recipe, with fish, is how I like it. If you have a good homemade vegetable or chicken stock to use, then do, but boiled water is fine. This is a recipe that requires your full attention throughout the cooking time, so don't get distracted! It's delicious topped with chilli oil.

SERVES 2
PREP TIME 5 MINUTES
COOK TIME 35–40 MINUTES

1.5–2l (3–4¼ pints) just-boiled water

1 carrot, peeled and very finely chopped

1 celery stick, very finely sliced

150g (5½oz) long grain rice, washed thoroughly and drained

2 tbsp vegetable oil

10g (¼oz) ginger, sliced into very thin matchsticks

1 large garlic clove, sliced into thin rounds

2 tsp salt

½ tsp chicken powder

1 tbsp oyster sauce

2 spring onions (scallions), green and white parts separated and finely sliced

2 sea bass fillets (approx. 180g/6¼oz) or any other white fish fillets, skin-on

2 tbsp Crispy Fried Shallots (see page 142 or store-bought) and oil

1 tsp white pepper

1 tbsp sesame oil

1 tsp Chilli Oil (see page 140 or store-bought), optional

Add 1.5 litres (3 pints) of hot water to a large saucepan and bring to the boil. Add the carrot and celery and, after 1 minute, add the rice. Cook over a high heat for 20 minutes, stirring regularly. Gradually top up the pan with the remaining 500ml (17fl oz) of water, as needed (the texture should be like a wet porridge rather than a risotto).

Heat the oil in a small frying pan over a medium–high heat. Fry the ginger for 30 seconds, then add the garlic and fry for 1 minute. Remove the pan from the heat.

After the rice has been cooking for 20 minutes, add the salt, chicken powder and oyster sauce. Cook for a further 10 minutes, stirring throughout and adding more water as necessary. Tip in the crispy garlic and ginger along with the oil from the pan, as well as the white parts of the spring onions. Add the fish, making sure it's completely submerged in the congee and cook for another 3 minutes.

Divide between bowls, and top with the crispy fried shallots and oil and the green parts of the spring onions. Season with white pepper and drizzle over the sesame oil and chilli oil, if using.

SAMBALS & EXTRAS

SAMBALS

This chapter includes a selection of sambals, pickles, chutneys and extra toppings that are used throughout the book – the recipes are straighforward and, once you've tasted them, you absolutely won't regret making them from scratch. Pictured from left to right: Basic Sambal (see page 132), Crispy Fried Shallots (see page 142), Mint and Coriander Chutney (see page 135), Ginger/Garlic Paste (see page 138), Spiced Pickle (see page 144) and the Roti King Special Spice Mix (see page 134).

BASIC SAMBAL VG

This chilli paste is integral to Malaysian cooking. Once you've made a batch, it can be added to many of the recipes in this book, saving you time. Hopefully you'll see its beauty as much as I do and you'll be keen to make it again. Pictured on the far-left on page 130.

Stick to the cooking times given and try not to rush the process – the sauce really needs to reduce down a lot for the sambal to work. Once you've made a batch, transfer it to a sterilized jar and store it in the fridge, where it will last for up to two weeks. You can also freeze half the batch to save for longer, if you wish.

MAKES 1 X 500G
(1LB 2OZ) JAR
PREP TIME 5 MINUTES
COOK TIME 50 MINUTES

40g (1½oz) whole dried Kashmiri chillies

180g (6¼oz) fresh red chillies, stalks removed

1 tbsp Ginger Paste (see page 138)

2 tbsp Garlic Paste (see page 138)

2 lemongrass sticks (approx. 30g/1oz), tops cut off and bottoms bashed and cut into small pieces

6 tbsp vegetable oil

2 large onions, finely chopped

3 tsp salt

Place a small pan of boiling water over a low heat. Add the dried chillies and soak for 5–10 minutes.

Once hydrated, drain them and add them to a blender along with the fresh chillies, ginger and garlic pastes, lemongrass, 2 tablespoons of the oil and 150ml (5fl oz) of water. Blend until smooth (depending on your blender, you will probably need to scrape down the sides in between blending). Add a dash more water if needed.

Heat the remaining 4 tablespoons of oil in a large pan over a medium heat. Add the onions and 2 teaspoons of the salt and cook for 10 minutes or until soft. Add the paste and cook over a low heat for 15 minutes, stirring frequently. Then add 100ml (3½fl oz) of water and cook for a further 15 minutes, still stirring often. You need to keep stirring to stop the mixture sticking on the bottom of the pan, and check the sambal isn't burning. The colour should have darkened after this time, which is a sign that the sambal is ready. Add the final 1 teaspoon of salt, then cook for a further 5–10 minutes or until the oil has separated and the sauce is a deep, dark red. Decant into a sterilized jar and when cool, refrigerate.

SAMBAL IKAN BILIS

ANCHOVY SAMBAL

60g (2¼oz) dried anchovies

150ml (5fl oz) vegetable oil

200g (7oz) basic sambal
  (see opposite page)

300ml (10fl oz) just-boiled water

1 large onion, finely sliced

5g (⅛oz) shrimp paste

1 tsp tamarind dissolved in 50ml
  (1½fl oz) just-boiled water

1 tsp sugar

1½ tsp salt

Use the basic sambal, opposite, to make this anchovy variation. This is mainly used for the Nasi Lemak spread (see page 52), but it is also delicious in the Sambal Ikan Bilis Croissant (see page 127).

Fry the dried anchovies in the oil over a low heat for 2–3 minutes until golden and crispy, then remove with a slotted spoon and set aside on paper towels, leaving the oil in the pan.

Place a bowl over a set of scales and measure out the basic sambal and the just-boiled water, then mix these together to make a paste.

Add the onions to the pan of oil, turn up the heat to high and fry until browned, which should take about 3 minutes. Turn the heat down to low and add the sambal paste to the pan with the onions, along with another 50ml (1½fl oz) water, the shrimp paste and the tamarind water. Stir through, add the sugar and salt and cook for 10–15 minutes.

ROTI KING SPECIAL SPICE MIX VG

<hr/>

This is my mum's secret recipe and we now use it in the Roti King restaurants – it took some persuading, but she eventually agreed to let me include it in the book! As a child I remember watching her as she'd toast the ingredients and then pound them by hand to a powder. She'd add a little of the powder into curries as they cooked, before adding a final little sprinkle just before serving up. It's important to add the spice mix both during cooking and after.

This spice mix is used in the Gulai Tumis (see page 40), Chicken Masala (see page 82), Varuval Crispy Potatoes (see page 106) and Hati Ayam Masak Pedas (see page 118).

MAKES 1 x 200ML (6¾FL OZ) JAR
PREP TIME 5 MINUTES
COOK TIME 15–20 MINUTES

40g (1½oz) white poppy seeds

20g (¾oz) whole dried Kashmiri chillies

30g (1oz) coriander seeds

30g (1oz) fennel seeds

5 curry leaves

In a large pan set over a low heat, toast the poppy seeds for 7 minutes, stirring often. Remove from the heat and put to one side.

In the same pan, toast the dried chillies, coriander and fennel seeds and curry leaves, stirring for 10 minutes or until the aromas are released. Once cool, add to a spice grinder, pestle and mortar or blender, along with the poppy seeds, and grind to a powder. Keep the spice mix in an airtight container for up to four months.

MINT AND CORIANDER CHUTNEY VG

This makes a punchy and delicious, smooth, bright green sauce that is a great addition to any banana leaf meal (see page 169).

MAKES 1 x 400G (14OZ) JAR
PREP TIME 15 MINUTES

100g (3½oz) fresh or frozen shredded coconut (see page 16 for preparation)

75g (2½oz) mint, leaves picked

75g (2½oz) coriander (cilantro), leaves picked

1 tbsp tamarind mixed with 2 tbsp water

1 tbsp vegetable oil

2 tsp lime juice

½ onion, roughly chopped

1 tsp Garlic Paste (see page 138)

1 fresh green chilli, stalk removed and roughly chopped

1 tsp salt

Use a blender to combine the coconut with the rest of the chutney ingredients, along with 75ml (2¼fl oz) of water. You should have a smooth green sauce (if it's not yet smooth, add a little more water, a tablespoon at a time). Taste the chutney, adding a further teaspoon of salt if needed.

Decant the chutney into a sterilized jar and keep refrigerated, where it will last up to three weeks.

GINGER/GARLIC PASTE VG

Ginger and garlic pastes are used so often in Malaysian cooking, so it's a good idea to make your own. When you have a jar of each in your fridge, it speeds up the preparation times for so many dishes. Scale the quantities here up or down as you wish.

MAKES 1 X 250G (9OZ)
JAR OF EACH
PREP TIME 10 MINUTES

150g (5½oz) garlic cloves, or 150g (5½oz) ginger, roughly chopped

2 tbsp vegetable oil

Add either the garlic or the ginger to a blender. Pour in the oil along with 70ml (2¼fl oz) of water and blend until smooth. Decant to an airtight container or a jar and store in the fridge for up to three weeks.

ONION MASALA PASTE VG

This paste is used for the chicken or lamb filling of the Roti Murtabak (see page 37), but it's very versatile. You could also use it as a base for any other meaty curry.

MAKES 1 X 500G
(1LB 2OZ) JAR
PREP TIME 5 MINUTES
COOK TIME 55 MINUTES

200ml (7fl oz) vegetable oil

6 onions, finely sliced

3 tsp salt

1 cinnamon stick

3 cardamom pods

10 curry leaves

2 tsp fennel seeds

1 star anise

2 cloves

2 tbsp Garlic Paste (see page 138)

2 tbsp Ginger Paste (see page 138)

150g (5½oz) curry powder

1 tbsp Kashmiri chilli powder

½ tsp turmeric powder

1 tbsp garam masala

Heat the oil in a large pan over a medium heat. Add the onions and salt and cook for 15 minutes or until soft, stirring often. Remove from the pan, blend until smooth (depending on your blender, you will probably need to scrape down the sides in between blending) and then return to the same pan.

Add the cinnamon stick, cardamom, curry leaves, fennel seeds, star anise and cloves and cook for a further 10 minutes, stirring often so the paste doesn't stick. Add a dash more water, if needed.

Lower the heat and add the garlic and ginger pastes and cook for a further 15 minutes. You need to keep stirring to stop the mixture sticking on the bottom of the pan, and check the paste isn't burning. Then add the curry powder, Kashmiri chilli powder, turmeric and garam masala and cook for a further 10 minutes along with 100ml (3½fl oz) water. Keep cooking on a low heat until the oil starts to separate.

Decant into a sterilized jar and when cool, refrigerate.

MY FAVOURITE CHILLI OIL

There are so many chilli oils available, with trusty brands such as Lee Kum Kee, now joined by lots of smaller-batch versions. Despite the choice out there, I really don't think you can beat making your own. This chilli oil will keep for up to six months, so a jar makes a great gift for friends. The uses for this sweet, salty and spicy chilli oil are endless. I particularly enjoy this on top of the Congee (see page 129) and I also rely on it to give extra flavour to instant noodles (when I'm in a rush and need something full of flavour to eat). This recipe will be one that you tweak to the tastes of you and your family and that you will keep making again and again. If you prefer a looser sauce, just add more oil as you go, to taste.

When you're preparing the ingredients, aim to chop them into roughly 1cm (½in) chunks.

MAKES APPROX. 1L
(4 X 250ML/8½FL OZ JARS)
PREP TIME 15 MINUTES
COOK TIME 25 MINUTES

550ml (18½fl oz) vegetable oil,
  plus 1 tbsp for frying

200g (7oz) banana shallots,
  roughly chopped

4 lemongrass sticks, white parts
  only, bashed and roughly chopped

100g (3½oz) dried Kashmiri chillies,
  roughly chopped

100g (3½oz) fresh red chillies, stalks
  removed, roughly chopped

100g (3½oz) ginger, roughly
  chopped

2 garlic bulbs, cloves roughly
  chopped

50g (1¾oz) dried shrimps, roughly
  chopped

50g (1¾oz) shrimp paste

juice of ½ lemon

50g (1¾oz) caster (superfine) sugar

2 tsp salt

Heat 1 tablespoon of oil in a large frying pan set over a low–medium heat. Add the shallots and cook for 5 minutes. Add the lemongrass, dried and fresh chillies, ginger, garlic, shrimps and shrimp paste, and cook for 7 minutes over a low heat, stirring frequently. The shallots should now have softened and the garlic will be starting to colour.

Remove from the heat and once slightly cooled, tip the contents of the pan into a blender along with half of the oil and blitz to a smooth paste – see the desired consistency opposite. Tip back into the pan and cook again for 15–20 minutes, until the colour darkens slightly and the oil separates.

Add the lemon juice, sugar and salt. Taste and check that the balance of sweet versus sour is to your taste. You could add more sugar or salt if you think necessary. Decant into a sterilized jar and pour over the remaining oil.

辣椒酱自便
CHILLI SAUCE SELF-SERVICE

BAWANG GORENG VG

CRISPY FRIED SHALLOTS

Lots of Malaysian street-food dishes are topped with crispy fried shallots. You can easily buy them ready-made, but if you'd like to make your own, they will stay fresh in an airtight container for up to a month. If you can get hold of round Asian shallots from specialist shops, do use them here, but if not, use regular round shallots, or the common banana variety will also work well. Use a mandolin or a sharp knife to evenly slice the shallots. You can scale this recipe up or down depending on how many crispy fried shallots you need.

MAKES 1 X 500G
(1LB 2OZ) JAR
PREP TIME 5 MINUTES
COOK TIME 10 MINUTES

400g (14oz) shallots

vegetable oil, for shallow-frying

½ tsp salt

Using a mandolin or a sharp knife, finely slice the shallots into rings about 1–2mm (1⁄16in) thick. Use paper towels to pat the shallot rings to remove any moisture before frying.

Heat 3cm (1in) of oil in a medium pan to 170°C (340°F). If you don't have a thermometer, test if the oil is hot enough by adding some of the shallots – the oil is ready when the shallots start to colour and become golden within 60 seconds. Fry the shallots in batches.

Use a strainer or slotted spoon (save the oil for later use) to remove the shallots, then tip straight onto paper towels to absorb the excess oil. Spread out the shallots so they have a chance to cool and crisp up, then season with the salt. Once completely cool, store in an airtight container and use generously to top your dishes.

ACHAR TIMUN VG

SPICED PICKLE

This delicious and vibrantly colourful pickle is great with Coconut Rice (see page 108) and Rendang (see page 54), but also pretty much anything else. It's sweet, sour and tangy and cuts through richer dishes, so it makes a perfect accompaniment to any banana leaf meal (see page 169).

MAKES 1 X 500G (1LB 2OZ) JAR
PREP TIME 10 MINUTES
COOK TIME 7 MINUTES

1 tbsp vegetable oil

3 star anise

½ cinnamon stick

½ tsp black mustard seeds

1 tsp Kashmiri chilli powder

300ml (10½fl oz) white vinegar

2 tsp salt

50g (1¾oz) caster (superfine) sugar

3 bay leaves

3 green bird's eye chillies, halved

2 red bird's eye chillies, halved

100g (3½oz) peanuts, toasted

1 tbsp sesame seeds, toasted

For the pickle

½ daikon radish (approx. 180g/6¼oz)

1 carrot, cut into batons

1 cucumber, seeds removed and cut into batons

½ white cabbage, shredded

4 garlic cloves, halved

2 baby shallots, finely sliced

200g (7oz) fresh pineapple, chopped into 2cm (¾in) chunks

For the paste

2 garlic cloves

2 baby shallots

15g (½oz) turmeric

Start making the pickle by adding all the prepared pickle ingredients to a 1-litre (35fl oz) jar or container.

To make the paste, add the ingredients along with a splash of water to a blender and blitz until smooth.

Pour the oil into a large pan and set over a medium–high heat. Add the star anise, cinnamon and mustard seeds. Let them sizzle for 2 minutes before adding the paste. Cook for 5 minutes, stirring constantly, then add the chilli powder. The mixture should now have thickened. Add the vinegar, salt and sugar, combine, then remove from the heat.

Add the bay leaves along with the green and red chillies to the top of the pickle jar before pouring over the liquid and its aromatics.

Using a pestle and mortar, bash together the toasted peanuts and sesame seeds before adding to the jar.

Seal the jar and leave to pickle for at least 24 hours, before giving the contents a stir to ensure they're well combined. Transfer to the fridge, where it'll keep for a month.

DESSERTS

PENCUCI MULUT

'Pencuci mulut' literally translates as 'mouth cleanser' – it's the traditional term in Malay-speaking countries for desserts. At the restaurant we have a simple desserts menu – including a selection of sweet roti with fillings or toppings and so I've included recipes for these on the following pages. In this chapter, you'll also find recipes for desserts that make use of leftover coconut milk from making roti canai, such as the No-churn Coconut and Pandan Ice Cream (see page 148) and the Chocolate Potong (see page 151), as well as recipes that celebrate ingredients used commonly in Malaysian cooking, like coconut, pandan and plantain.

NO-CHURN COCONUT PANDAN ICE CREAM v

I learned how to make smooth, scoopable ice cream without needing an ice-cream churner here in the UK – it's really easy! This recipe is a great way to use up the leftover condensed milk you might have after making the Roti Canai (see page 35). If you can't get hold of fresh pandan leaves, you could either use pandan essence (which will give you a vibrant green colour, though not that great a flavour) or just leave it out altogether – it will still be delicious. This ice cream can be enjoyed on its own and is also lovely alongside the Pisang Goreng (see page 154) or the Cekodok Pisang (see page 153).

MAKES 1 X 1-LITRE (35FL OZ) TUB
PREP TIME 15 MINUTES, PLUS 4 HOURS OR OVERNIGHT FREEZING TIME

10 fresh pandan leaves, roughly chopped

500ml (17fl oz) double (heavy) cream

250g (9oz) condensed milk

200ml (7fl oz) coconut milk

50g (1¾oz) fresh or frozen shredded coconut (see page 16 for preparation)

toasted coconut flakes, to serve (optional)

Bring a small saucepan of water to the boil. Add the pandan leaves and after 30 seconds, drain them from the water. Transfer to a blender and blitz with 100ml (3½fl oz) of cold water. Strain this mixture through a muslin cloth or a very fine sieve and you will be left with a small amount of bright green liquid.

In a large bowl whisk the cream to very soft peaks, being careful not to over-whisk. Pour in the condensed milk, coconut milk and the pandan liquid, and whisk again until fully incorporated. Stir through the shredded coconut.

Pour the mixture into a freezable container and freeze for a minimum of 4 hours or ideally overnight.

When ready to serve, scatter over toasted coconut flakes, if you like.

LEMON ICED TEA POTONG VG

ⅿⅿⅿⅿⅿⅿⅿⅿ

In Malaysia, ice lollies are sold as a refreshing snack from roadside sellers pretty much everywhere. Red bean and coconut is a popular flavour combination, but here I've decided to include chocolate along with a refreshing lemon iced-tea lolly, as my children love both of these variations. Potong means 'to cut' in Malay, because traditionally each flavour is made in a large, oblong block and the lollies are cut up smaller to sell. When I make these I use plastic pop-ice bags, tying the ends before freezing, but use whichever moulds you have.

SERVES 6–8 DEPENDING
ON MOULD SIZE
PREP TIME 10 MINUTES,
PLUS OVERNIGHT FREEZING

5 English breakfast tea bags

90g (3¼oz) caster (superfine) sugar

juice of 2 lemons

½ lemon, finely sliced into half
  moons

small handful of mint leaves, finely
  sliced

Place the tea bags into a large heatproof jug and pour over 430ml (14½fl oz) of boiling water. Add the sugar and stir to dissolve. Leave to brew for 5 minutes.

Remove the tea bags. Add the lemon juice, then taste to check the sweetness, adding more lemon juice or sugar to your taste. Leave it to cool completely before adding the lemon slices and mint, then decant into the moulds and freeze overnight.

CHOCOLATE POTONG V

MAKES 6–8 DEPENDING
ON MOULD SIZE
PREP TIME 5 MINUTES,
PLUS OVERNIGHT FREEZING

120g (4¼oz) chocolate malt drink
  powder

100g (3½oz) condensed milk

I use Milo, the chocolate-flavoured malted powder, to make these chocolate ice lollies.

In a large jug, whisk together all the ingredients, along with 250ml (9fl oz) of boiling water, until smooth. Pour into ice lolly moulds and freeze overnight.

CEKODOK PISANG VG

BANANA FRITTERS WITH CINNAMON SUGAR

This is a popular street-food snack in Malaysia and a good way of using up very ripe bananas. The cinnamon sugar is a delicious addition to these vegan treats. These fritters are best eaten on the day they're made, and better yet, while still warm.

MAKES 18–20
PREP TIME 10 MINUTES
COOK TIME 20–30 MINUTES

vegetable oil, for frying

300g (10½oz) very ripe bananas, peeled

1 tsp vanilla bean paste

140g (5oz) plain (all-purpose) flour

1 tsp baking powder

1 tsp caster (superfine) sugar

1 tbsp dark soft brown sugar

½ tsp ground cinnamon

½ tsp salt

For the cinnamon sugar

1 tbsp caster (superfine) sugar

1 tsp ground cinnamon

Half-fill a medium saucepan with oil and place over a high heat.

While the oil is getting hot, make the batter. In a medium bowl, mash together the bananas and the vanilla paste with a fork. Whisk together the flour, baking powder, sugars, cinnamon and salt before adding to the banana mixture.

Prepare the cinnamon sugar by adding the sugar and cinnamon to a small tray or shallow bowl.

The oil should have heated to 170°C (350°F). If you don't have a thermometer, you can test whether it's hot enough by dropping in a very small amount of batter – it should sizzle as it meets the oil and start to colour in 20 seconds. Drop a small tablespoonful worth of the batter into the oil and fry for 2–3 minutes until golden. Repeat until the batter is all used up (you may need to fry in batches).

Remove the fritters with a slotted spoon and drain on paper towels before tossing in the cinnamon sugar to coat.

PISANG GORENG ^{VG}

BATTERED PLANTAIN

You find these simple, sweet snacks at night markets in Ipoh. My wife Kalpana likes to cook these for my children, and they're best eaten warm.

SERVES 4–6
PREP TIME 10 MINUTES
COOK TIME 15 MINUTES

60g (2¼oz) self-raising (self-rising) flour

60g (2¼oz) plain (all-purpose) flour

1 tbsp rice flour

¼ tsp ground turmeric

¼ tsp salt

2 tsp caster (superfine) sugar

vegetable oil, for shallow-frying

2 medium very ripe plantains, sliced into thin slices approx. 10cm (4in) long

Whisk together all the flours, turmeric, salt and sugar in a large bowl before slowly adding 150ml (5½fl oz) of water, combining as you go. Keep whisking until the batter is smooth and lump-free.

Place a small frying pan over a high heat and add enough oil to fill it to a depth of 2cm (¾in). Once the oil is hot, dip the plantain slices into the batter to coat before adding them to the pan. Fry in batches so that you don't overcrowd the pan – the plantains need space or they'll stick together. Fry for 2–3 minutes, turning them in the hot oil to cook on both sides. Remove from the pan with a slotted spoon, then drain on paper towels before eating them warm. I like to eat these with coconut ice cream (see page 148).

SWEET ROTI

Sweet roti canai are a very popular Malaysian street food and a real favourite at Roti King, too. Using the Roti Canai dough, here are two variations of sweet roti to try. Follow the method on page 35 to make the dough, then once the roti has been stretched, the sweet filling can be added (similar to the method for making Roti Murtabak on page 37) before being cooked.

Each of the upcoming recipes requires one ball of roti dough. If you have made a full batch of roti (ten portions) it's a great idea to save some dough balls to experiment with these sweet variations.

PLANTA v
SERVES 1

1 Roti Canai (see page 35)

1 tsp butter

1 tsp soft dark brown sugar

2 tbsp condensed milk

Sweet roti served with condensed milk is another popular snack sold by street vendors in Malaysia – see picture, opposite.

First, follow the method for Roti Canai on pages 35–36.

Place the stretched-out roti on a plate, spread the butter on top and sprinkle over the sugar. Fold the roti and drizzle over the condensed milk.

PISANG v
SERVES 1

1 Roti Canai (see page 35)

½ banana, finely sliced

1 tsp jaggery

1 tsp soft dark brown sugar

Sweet roti with banana is a traditional dessert, often made in Malaysia with white sugar, though I prefer a mix of brown sugar and jaggery, which I think gives a better flavour and caramelization. If you can't get hold of jaggery, just double the brown sugar. Traditionally, roti pisang has an egg mixed with the banana, but I prefer just banana and that's how I serve it at Roti King.

First, follow the method for Roti Canai on pages 35–36.

Across the surface of the stretched-out roti, spread the banana slices, then sprinkle over the jaggery and sugar. Fold the roti over into a square shape.

DRINKS

MINUMAN

This chapter is a celebration of classic Malaysian drinks – you'll find all of these served at cafés and stalls across the country and each family will have their own closely guarded recipe. Some of these are even a spectacle to watch being made, see the recipe and techniques for 'pulled tea' on pages 162–165.

TEH O'AIS LIMAU [VG]
ROTI KING ICED LEMON TEA

You can make this as sweet as you like – just taste and add more sugar towards the end. Don't leave it to steep for much longer than 10 minutes or it will over brew.

SERVES 1
PREP TIME 10 MINUTES

1 English breakfast tea bag

3–4 tsp caster (superfine) sugar

½ small unwaxed lemon

ice, to serve

In a small jug, brew the tea bag in 150ml (5fl oz) boiling water, leaving it to steep for 5–10 minutes. Stir through 3 teaspoons of the sugar. Squeeze over 1 tablespoon of lemon juice (using a sieve to catch any pips), then add the squeezed lemon half to the tea, too. Taste, adding another teaspoon of sugar if you would like it sweeter, or more lemon to make it sharper. Serve over ice.

TEH AIS _v

ROTI KING ICED COFFEE

Similar to pulled tea, this iced coffee uses both condensed and evaporated milk and gives a sweet caffeine hit that also helps to cool you down in the midday heat. The 'pulling' method involves pouring the liquid back and forth between a jug and a cup. This action helps to create a frothy, bubbly drink while also cooling the coffee down, so that when you add the ice it won't immediately melt and dilute the coffee.

SERVES 1
PREP TIME 5 MINUTES

1 tsp instant coffee

2 tsp evaporated milk

4 tsp condensed milk

ice, to serve

Mix the coffee and both milks in a small jug, adding 100ml (3½fl oz) of boiling water. Taste and adjust accordingly. Pour the milky coffee between the jug and a cup at least five times.

Prepare a cold glass full of ice. Pour the coffee over the ice and drink straight away.

TEH TARIK V

ROTI KING PULLED TEA

Milky sweet tea is served all over south-east Asia, and the Malaysian version uses both condensed and evaporated milk. A popular street-vendor drink, it's pulled between two vessels to froth it and there are a variety of techniques used, including different lengths of 'pull' that subtly change the temperature and taste of the brew. This recipe is a staple at Roti King and can be served either very hot or cold over ice (both are worth trying). If serving cool, you can pre-mix the tea and keep it in a jug to pour over ice when you're ready to serve.

SERVES 2
PREP TIME 7 MINUTES

2 English breakfast tea bags

1 tsp evaporated milk

3 tsp condensed milk

Brew the tea bags in 130ml (4½fl oz) of boiling water, leaving them to steep for a minimum of 5 minutes. Remove the tea bags and pour in both milks. Shake the tea and 'pull' it to make it frothy. You could use a hand blender for this but I like to pull by hand as per the technique back home. Serve hot or over ice.

LIMAU AIS VG

HOMEMADE LIME AND LEMONADE

This is a refreshing drink that's easy to make with any mix of citrus you have – I particularly like using some limes alongside the lemons. I find that light brown sugar gives a slightly more interesting flavour than white. It can be made ahead of time and kept in the fridge, then when you're ready to serve, mix it with sparkling water and serve over ice with lemon slices and mint leaves. It's perfect on a hot day – and even better if there's a barbecue on the go.

SERVES 4–6
PREP TIME 15 MINUTES

6 unwaxed lemons

120g (4¼oz) light brown sugar

juice of 3 limes

pinch of fine sea salt (optional)

sparkling water, to serve

ice, to serve

lemon or lime slices and mint leaves, to serve

Peel the lemons with a vegetable peeler and add the strips of peel to a medium saucepan. Add the sugar and 500ml (17fl oz) of water, bring to the boil, then take off the heat and leave to cool.

In the meantime, squeeze the juice from the peeled lemons and the limes. Once the liquid in the pan is cool, strain to remove the peel and add the juice of the lemons and the limes to the liquid. Taste and adjust the sweetness, adding more sugar if you like or a small pinch of salt.

To serve, mix with sparkling water and serve over ice with a lemon or lime slice before topping with a few torn mint leaves.

BANANA LEAF MEAL

NASI DAUN PISANG

Our family restaurant – Gopal's Corner in Ipoh – was famous for banana leaf meals. These are traditional south Indian celebration meals, usually vegetarian, but our Malaysian interpretation adds fish and meat. These are feasting menus to be enjoyed on special occasions with family and friends. The variety of curries should be paired together to cover sweet, sour and spicy.

To create a Malaysian-style banana leaf meal at home, you can cook the following recipes from this book:

- **Kari Kepala Ikan (Padma's fish-head curry – see page 66)**

- **Sambal Udang (prawn sambal – see page 75)**

- **Buntong Kacang Panjang (Buntong green beans – see page 110)**

- **Cabbage Poriyal (see page 115)**

- **Mint and Coriander Chutney (see page 135)**

- **Achar Timun (spiced pickle – see page 144)**

- **Serve with white basmati rice, cooked according to packet instructions**

INDEX

ABOUT THE AUTHOR & ACKNOWLEDGEMENTS

Sugen Gopal was born and raised in Ipoh, Malaysia, where in the family restaurant, his parents showcased their love of authentic Malaysian cuisine. Inspired by the food of his childhood, Sugen moved to London to open the first Roti King, serving a simple menu of Malaysian classics. For almost a decade, the restaurant has served its iconic Roti Canai at affordable prices to foodies in the know and, since then, Roti King has launched multiple sites and market stalls across the city. Often listed as the 'best roti in London', you'll find it featured in the *The Guardian, The Standard, the Independent, Eater, Time Out, delicious.* and more.

I owe special thanks in particular to my family. Firstly, thanks to my parents. Mum, you have always been my inspiration and dad, you are my backbone. To my wife, Kalpana, thank you for everything that you do and all of your support to help me achieve my dreams. Uncle Kanna and my brother, Suman – thank you for everything.

Thank you also to the people who have helped me with all things Roti King along the way: Panir, both Mr Lims and Nara.

Ganan, thank you for making my Roti King dreams a reality.

Lastly, to all my team, past and present. People call me the Roti King but without your dedication to food quality, your obsessive work ethic and your passion to please customers, there is no Roti King. Much love and thanks to you all.

Quadrille, Penguin Random House UK, One Embassy Gardens, 8 Viaduct Gardens, London SW11 7BW

Quadrille Publishing Limited is part of the Penguin Random House group of companies whose addresses can be found at global.penguinrandomhouse.com

Penguin
Random House
UK

Published by Quadrille in 2025

www.penguin.co.uk

A CIP catalogue record for this book is available from the British Library

ISBN 978 1 83783 211 8
10 9 8 7 6 5 4 3 2 1

Colour reproduction by F1

Printed in China by C&C Offset Printing Co., Ltd.

The authorised representative in the EEA is Penguin Random House Ireland, Morrison Chambers, 32 Nassau Street, Dublin D02 YH68.

Penguin Random House is committed to a sustainable future for our business, our readers and our planet. This book is made from Forest Stewardship Council® certified paper.

Managing Director Sarah Lavelle
Senior Commissioning Editor Stacey Cleworth
Editorial Assistant Ellie Spence
Writing Support and Recipe Development El Kemp
Designer Katy Everett
Photographer Sam Folan
Photographer's Assistant Gizem Kumbaraci and Allegra D'Agostini
Illustrations Design by Temple
Props Stylist Faye Wears
Food Stylist El Kemp
Food Stylist Assistants Aine Pretty-McGrath and Georgia Rudd
Head of Production Stephen Lang
Production Manager Sabeena Atchia
Production Controller Sumayyah Waheed